# ALTO SAXOPHONE

with contributions by
Larry Teal

# Do It!

## Play and Teach Woodwinds

### A Musical Text for Secondary Instrument Courses with a "Focus on Teaching"

## James O. Froseth

Molly A. Weaver, Contributing Editor

| Instrument | Book and CD |
|---|---|
| **Woodwind** | |
| Flute | M587 |
| Clarinet | M588 |
| Oboe | M589 |
| Bassoon | M590 |
| Alto Sax | M591 |
| Woodwind Teacher's Edition | M592 |
| **Brass** | |
| Trumpet | M595 |
| Horn in F | M596 |
| Trombone | M597 |
| Euphonium/Baritone | M598 |
| Tuba | M599 |
| Brass Teacher's Edition | M600 |

# Index to "FOCUS ON TEACHING"



# GETTING IT "RIGHT" FROM THE START
## Table of Contents



# GETTING IT "RIGHT" FROM THE START
## CD Index

# Index to Music Repertoire



# Index to Supplementary Resources

## GOALS AND OBJECTIVES

*Alto Saxophone Home Helper* has two primary goals: 1) to provide students with the home help needed to develop exemplary performance habits and practice procedures from the start, and 2) to transform early success playing the alto saxophone into a lifetime of musical enjoyment and participation.

**Objective 1:**

To exhibit all the performance skills represented by the player in the photograph.

**Step 1:**

Look carefully at the photograph to develop a mental image of the physical set-up you will need to be a successful alto saxophone player.

**Objective 2:**

To sound as much like the player on the CD as possible.

**Step 2:**

Listen to Track 1 on your *Play and Teach* CD to develop an overall concept of the task you are about to undertake.

# FOCUS ON TEACHING

## You Know You Are Prepared to Teach When You Are Able to:

- **Predict** exactly what you want to see and hear at the conclusion of every lesson or rehearsal

- **Discriminate** differences between what you are predicting and what you are seeing and hearing during each lesson or rehearsal

- **Remediate** deficiencies that you see and hear

Note: Abilities to predict expected outcomes, discriminate differences, and remediate deficiencies represent teaching skill and lesson planning at the highest level.

Suggestion: Employ the *Visual Diagnostic Skills Program* for Brass (M-536) and Woodwinds (M-537) to develop your abilities to visually predict, discriminate, and remediate.  www.giamusic.com

Suggestion: Employ the artist models on *Do It! Play and Teach* CDs to develop your abilities to aurally predict, discriminate, and remediate.

## KEYS TO SUCCESS

STUDENT – You will be much more likely to succeed if you:

1) take proper care of your instrument,
2) read every word of the text and follow all instructions,
3) practice with the CD every day,
4) follow the lead of your teacher, and
5) attend every lesson at school equipped to play and prepared to learn.


HOME HELPER – You will be most helpful to your student if you:

1) help your student to take proper care of the instrument,
2) read every word of the text,
3) monitor practice sessions regularly,
4) encourage your student to practice with the CD every day,
5) check off each achievement on every CHECKLIST once each week (remember, every check is a motivating "pat on the back"),
6) avoid negative comments,
7) give your student lots of attention, and
8) communicate with the teacher through your *Home Helper* book when questions or concerns arise.


TEACHER – You will be most helpful to your student if you:

1) recognize and record student achievement, and
2) coordinate the home helper's efforts with school instruction.

# FOCUS ON TEACHING

## What Are the Predictors of Music Achievement Prior to the Start of Instruction?

- Past achievement is the best predictor of future achievement.
- Students who move well to music are more likely to be successful instrumentalists than students who do not.
- Students who sing well are more likely to be successful instrumentalists than students who do not.
- Students who play an instrument such as recorder, piano, or guitar are more likely to be successful instrumentalists than students who do not.

## What Are the Predictors of Music Achievement After the Start of Instruction?

- Physical compatibility with the chosen instrument
- Quality of instrument
- Quality of instruction
- Opportunities to pursue self-determined musical interests
- Self-motivation
- Home help

# CARE OF THE ALTO SAXOPHONE

*The Alto Saxophone*

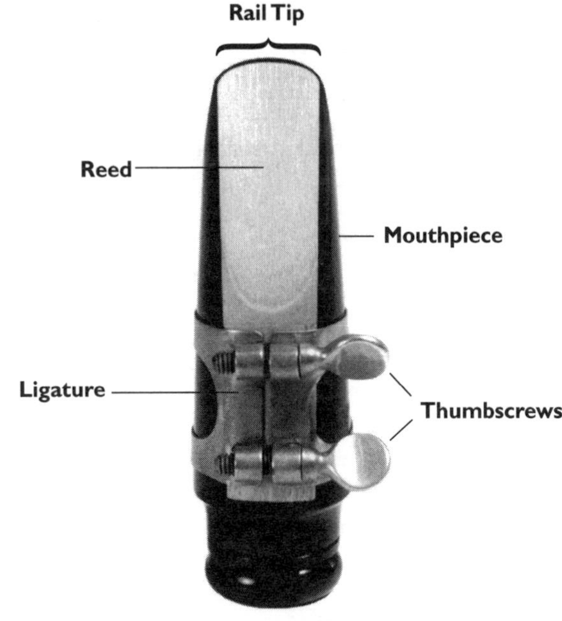



*The Reed and Mouthpiece Assembly*

Your alto saxophone is a fragile instrument that requires special care. Satisfactory progress is possible only if your instrument is in proper playing condition. If anything should go wrong with your saxophone, DO NOT ATTEMPT YOUR OWN REPAIRS. Only a qualified repair person has the experience and skill to service your saxophone. If you need advice, consult your teacher or your music dealer.

Proper instrument care begins with clean teeth and clean hands. Always brush your teeth after eating and before playing to avoid blowing food particles into your instrument. Also, wash your hands before handling your instrument. Clean hands will help to keep dirt out of the mechanisms of your instrument. Clean hands will also help to preserve the lacquer finish on your saxophone.

Before opening your saxophone case, place it on a flat surface and check carefully to see that you have it positioned with the lid upward. Your instrument might be damaged if you open the case upside down. Mark the lid of your case with tape if it is difficult to tell the top from the bottom.

After each time you play your instrument, disassemble it and return it to the case. Then, run a swab through the neck and the body two or three times to remove any moisture. Failure to swab regularly may result in damage to the pads on your saxophone. Wash the mouthpiece in lukewarm soapy water, rinse, and wipe dry with a soft cloth at least once a week.

Keep your saxophone in its case when not in use to avoid accidental damage. Always secure the latches after you close the lid. Do not force books, music, CD cases, or other items into the case on top of your instrument or beside it. Avoid exposing your saxophone to extreme heat or cold, moisture or excessive humidity, sharp blows, vibration, dust, dirt, or other possible sources of damage.

## GUIDELINES FOR PRODUCTIVE PRACTICE

**Guiding principle: Practice must have purpose.**

Step 1: Decide what it is you want to accomplish. For example:

1. **"I want to improve my:"**
   A. Embouchure (pages 8, 9, 10, and 11)
   B. Posture and Instrument Position (page 15)
   C. Left Hand Position (page 16)
   D. Right Hand Position (page 16)

2. **"I want to sound more like the model on the CD when I play on my mouthpiece and neck."**
   (Track 2 on pages 8 and 11)

3. **"I want to improve my articulation."** (Tracks 4 and 5 on page 13)

4. **"I want to sound more like the player on the CD when I play on my assembled saxophone."**
   (Track 6 on page 17, track 8 on page 18, and track 10 on page 19)

5. **"I want to improve my ability to play the call and response."**
   (Track 7 on page 17, track 9 on page 18, track 11 on page 19, and track 12 on page 20)

6. **"I want to sound more like the player on the CD when I play *Practice Every Day March*."**
   (Track 1 on page 20)

7. **"I want to breathe and phrase more like the player on the CD."** (Track 1 on page 20)

## RECOMMENDATIONS

1. Schedule several short practice sessions daily rather than one extended session.

2. Take frequent breaks during practice sessions to avoid fatigue.

3. Be spontaneous. Practice whenever you feel motivated to make music or improve your performance skills.

4. Encourage your adult home helper to oversee your practice as often as possible.

5. Schedule a regular weekly session for your adult home helper to enter achievement marks on every CHECKLIST.

# FOCUS ON TEACHING
## A Strategy for Teaching Music Performance

- Determine the Need for Instruction
  - New Material
  - Deficiencies Revealed through Ongoing Assessment of Student Performance
    Teacher Assessment
    Self-Assessment
    Peer Assessment
    Adult Home Helper Assessment

- Show Students the Specific Objective
        "It Sounds Like"
        "It Looks Like"

- Teach to the Objective
  - New Material: Teach and Evaluate the Effects of Instruction
  - Deficiencies Revealed through Assessment: Remediate and Evaluate the Effects of Remedial Instruction

Suggestion: Regularly employ *Band Home Helper* photographs and CD artist models to direct students' attention to specific music performance objectives.  www.giamusic.com

## THE MOUTHPIECE, NECK, LIGATURE, AND REED ASSEMBLY

**Step 1:** Grease the neck cork occasionally and only when necessary.

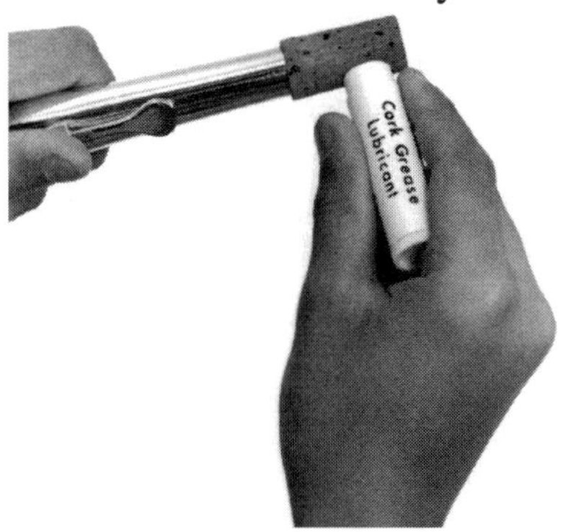


**Step 2:** Put the mouthpiece on the neck with a gentle back-and-forth turning motion.

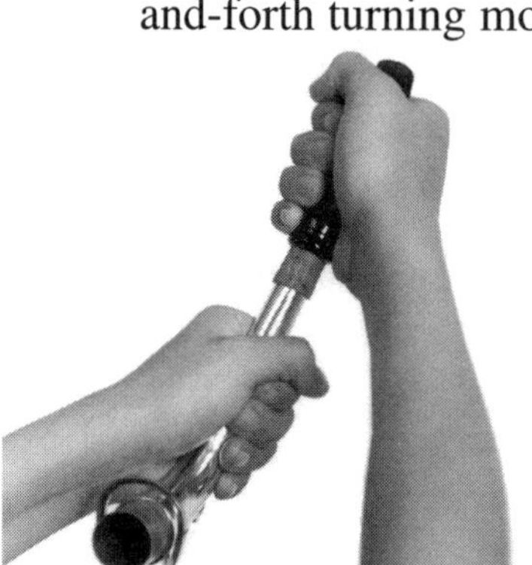

**Step 3:** Position the ligature over the mouthpiece.

**Step 4:** Push the ligature forward with the thumb and slip the reed between the ligature and the mouthpiece.

*Note: Handle the reed carefully. The tip is very delicate.*

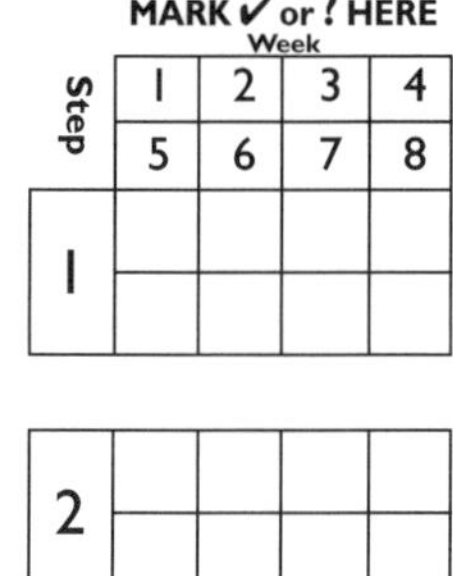
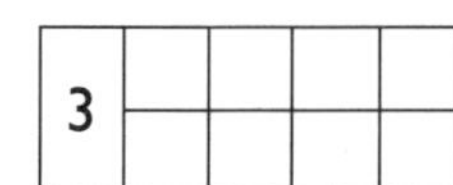
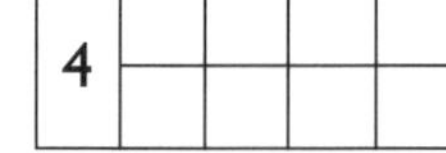

MARK ✔ or ? HERE

| Step | Week 1 | 2 | 3 | 4 |
|------|--------|---|---|---|
|      | 5 | 6 | 7 | 8 |
| 1 |  |  |  |  |
|   |  |  |  |  |
| 2 |  |  |  |  |
|   |  |  |  |  |
| 3 |  |  |  |  |
|   |  |  |  |  |
| 4 |  |  |  |  |
|   |  |  |  |  |

# FOCUS ON TEACHING

## Assessment Informs and Motivates

- Assessment Provides Students with Vital Feedback
  - Assessment is a means to recognize and reward achievement
  - Assessment establishes need for practice
  - Assessment determines specific objectives for practice

Suggestion: Use checklists to recognize and record achievement. Employ teacher assessment, self-assessment, peer assessment, and adult home helper assessment.

**Step 5:** Carefully slip the reed between the ligature and the mouthpiece.

**Step 6:** Align the tip of the reed with the mouthpiece rail tip and slide the ligature firmly down on the reed.

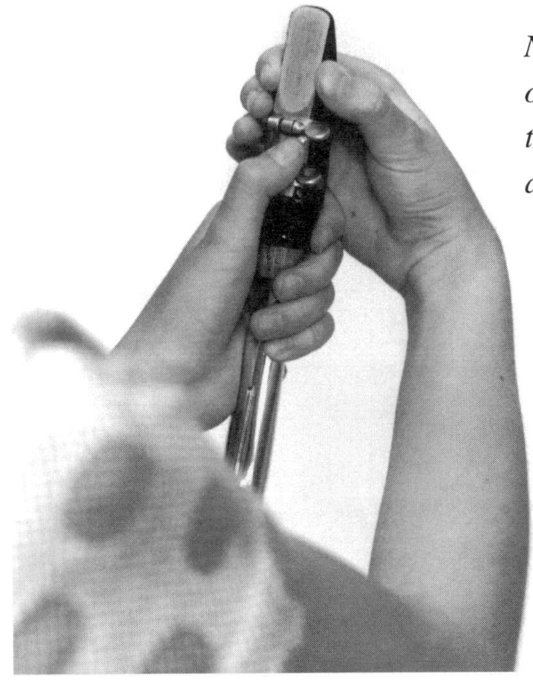

*Note: A thin ridge of mouthpiece rail tip should show above the reed.*

**Step 7:** Gently tighten the thumb screws.

*Note: The screws should be no tighter than necessary to hold the reed firmly in place.*

**Step 8:** Place the cap on the mouthpiece very carefully.

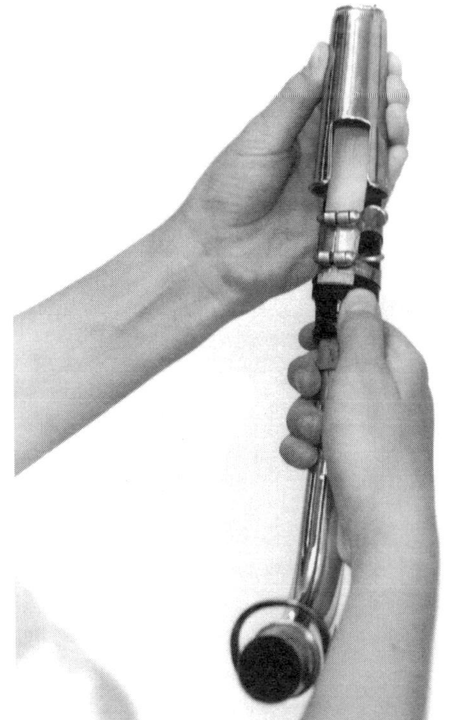

| Step | MARK ✔ or ? HERE Week | | | |
|---|---|---|---|---|
| | 1 | 2 | 3 | 4 |
| | 5 | 6 | 7 | 8 |
| 5 | | | | |
| 6 | | | | |
| 7 | | | | |
| 8 | | | | |

## FIRST TONES ON THE MOUTHPIECE-NECK ASSEMBLY

# *TRY THIS FIRST*

### • SOUNDS LIKE:

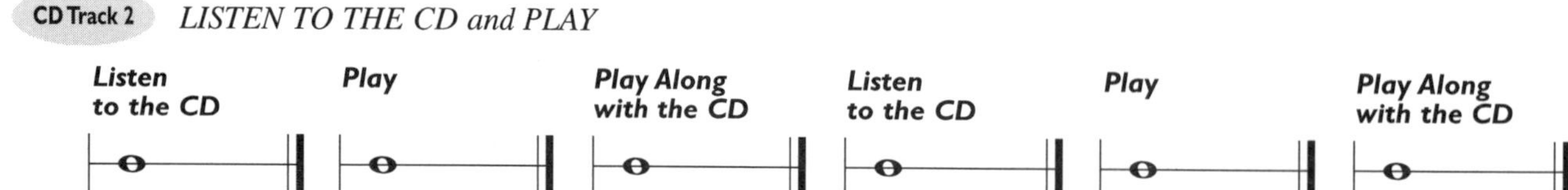


### • LOOKS LIKE

Many students will form an acceptable embouchure with a simple photographic representation of the embouchure and a recorded model of the sound made on the mouthpiece-neck assembly.

Too much verbal information can confuse your student and lead to mental overload.

To assess your student's embouchure refer to page 7 for a checklist of physical characteristics that define an acceptable alto saxophone embouchure.

To take your student through a step-by-step formation of the embouchure turn to pages 10 and 11.

# FOCUS ON TEACHING

## Helping Students Make the Best Choice of Instrument

- Every student has unique physical characteristics.
- Some students have physical characteristics that are not well suited to their first choice of instrument.
- Finding the best physical match can be the difference between success and failure.

Suggested Procedure: Use the photographs, CD sound tracks, and suggested procedures contained in "Choosing for Success," *Teacher's Reference and Resource Edition, Home Helper for Band* to aid students in making the best choice of instrument.  www.giamusic.com

# KEY ELEMENTS OF THE ALTO SAXOPHONE EMBOUCHURE

The word "embouchure" (ahm-bu-shure) refers to the position and use of the lips and facial muscles to produce a tone on a wind instrument.

✔ **If Satisfactory**     **?** **If More Work Is Needed**

A. The upper teeth are on top of the mouthpiece approximately 1/2 inch down from the rail tip.

B. A cushion of lower lip covers the lower teeth.

C. The lips are sealed inward around the mouthpiece with equal support from every direction.

D. A natural concavity is visible between the lower lip and chin.

E. The upper and lower teeth are comfortably aligned.

F. The mouthpiece is placed to the center of the mouth at a downward angle.

G. The tone and pitch match the CD. (If the tone and pitch produced by the student do not match the CD, check the amount of mouthpiece placed into the mouth. Too much mouthpiece into the mouth will produce a harsh, honky sound; too little will produce a small, pinched sound.)

**MARK ✔ or ? HERE**

| Step | Week 1 | 2 | 3 | 4 |
|------|---|---|---|---|
|      | 5 | 6 | 7 | 8 |
| A |  |  |  |  |
| B |  |  |  |  |
| C |  |  |  |  |
| D |  |  |  |  |
| E |  |  |  |  |
| F |  |  |  |  |
| G |  |  |  |  |

# FOCUS ON TEACHING
## Positive Teaching versus Negative Teaching

- A positive instructional statement defines the objective and focuses the student's attention on the desired behavior.

  *"Seal your lips around the mouthpiece with equal support from every direction."*

- A negative instructional statement does not define the objective nor does it focus the student's attention on the desired behavior.

  *"Don't puff your cheeks out."*

Suggestion: Use the positive models and descriptions in *Alto Saxophone Home Helper* to focus students' attention on desired performance behavior. www.giamusic.com

## FORMING THE ALTO SAXOPHONE EMBOUCHURE - STEP-BY-STEP

**Step 1:** Position your upper teeth on top of the mouthpiece approximately 1/2 inch down from the tip.

*Note: The mouthpiece should be positioned to the center of your mouth at the downward angle displayed in the photograph.*

| MARK ✔ or ? HERE | | | |
| --- | --- | --- | --- |

| | Week | | | |
| --- | --- | --- | --- | --- |
| | 1 | 2 | 3 | 4 |
| Step | 5 | 6 | 7 | 8 |
| 1 | | | | |

**Step 2:** Cover your lower teeth with a cushion of lower lip.

| 2 | | | |
| --- | --- | --- | --- |
| | | | |

**Step 3:** Take a full breath of air in through your mouth.

*Note: It is virtually impossible to take a full breath of air in through your nose.*

**Step 4:** Seal your lips around the mouthpiece by pushing the corners of your mouth inward toward the center of the mouthpiece.

*Note: Your upper and lower teeth should be comfortably aligned, and your embouchure muscles should be drawn into a smooth, firm circle around the mouthpiece with equal support from every direction.*

*Note: A concavity should be visible between your lower lip and chin.*

## PLAYING ON THE MOUTHPIECE-NECK ASSEMBLY

**CD Track 2**  *LISTEN TO THE CD and PLAY*

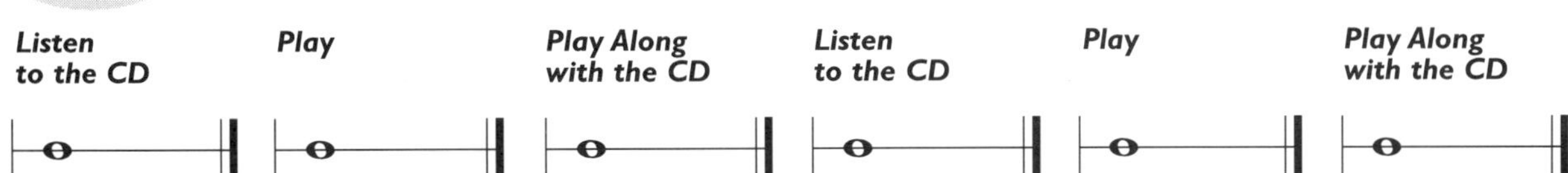


**Step 5:** Learn to produce a long tone by blowing a steady stream of air into the mouthpiece-neck assembly.

*Caution: Too much pressure on the reed from your lower jaw will stifle the vibration of the reed and produce a tone that sounds pinched.*

*Caution: Loose lips that are not sealed toward the center of the mouthpiece will produce an unpleasant tone that is also flat in pitch.*

*Caution: Loose lips that are not sealed toward the center of the mouth can also result in puffed cheeks.*

# FOCUS ON TEACHING
## Positive Reinforcement versus Negative Reinforcement

- A positive reinforcement uses words or actions to indicate approval of a student's response to a teacher initiative.

  Teacher initiative: "Now we're going to listen to the CD and play on the mouthpiece-neck assembly. Ready?"
  Positive reinforcement: "Good effort. Try again. This time seal your lips around the mouthpiece with equal support from every direction......... That's right!"

Suggestion: Use positive reinforcement to acknowledge both effort and achievement.

- A negative reinforcement uses words or actions to indicate disapproval of a student's response to a teacher initiative.

  Teacher initiative: "Now we're going to listen and play on the mouthpiece-neck assembly. Ready?"
  Negative reinforcement: "Tom, is that the best you can do?"

  Note: A negative reinforcement acknowledges neither effort nor achievement.

Suggestion: Avoid negative reinforcement.

# MUSICAL ARTICULATION

Articulation refers to how the tone is started and how it is stopped. This important aspect of instrumental performance requires correct posture, correct breathing and breath control, and a good embouchure.

### Starting the Tone

A tone is started when a stream of air from the lungs sets the reed vibrating. The tongue acts as the valve that releases the airstream into the mouthpiece. Figure 1 below shows the position of the tongue on the tip of the reed prior to the start of the tone. Figure 2 illustrates the position of the tongue after the tone has begun. *NOTE: The lower jaw remains stable while tonguing.*

### Stopping the Tone

There are two acceptable ways to stop a tone. The first is by stopping the airstream. This method is used at the end of a long tone, before a silence in the music, and for separated styles of articulation. Pronounce the syllables "tu," "tu," "tu," "tu," with a space after each syllable to simulate this style of articulation. The second way to stop the tone is by simply touching the tip edge of the reed quickly and lightly with the tongue. This method is used for fast tonguing and for a connected style of articulation. To simulate this style of articulation pronounce the syllables "du–du–du–du–" with the sensation that the airflow is continuous. Avoid articulation that sounds like the syllables "thu," "hu," "thut," or "hutt."

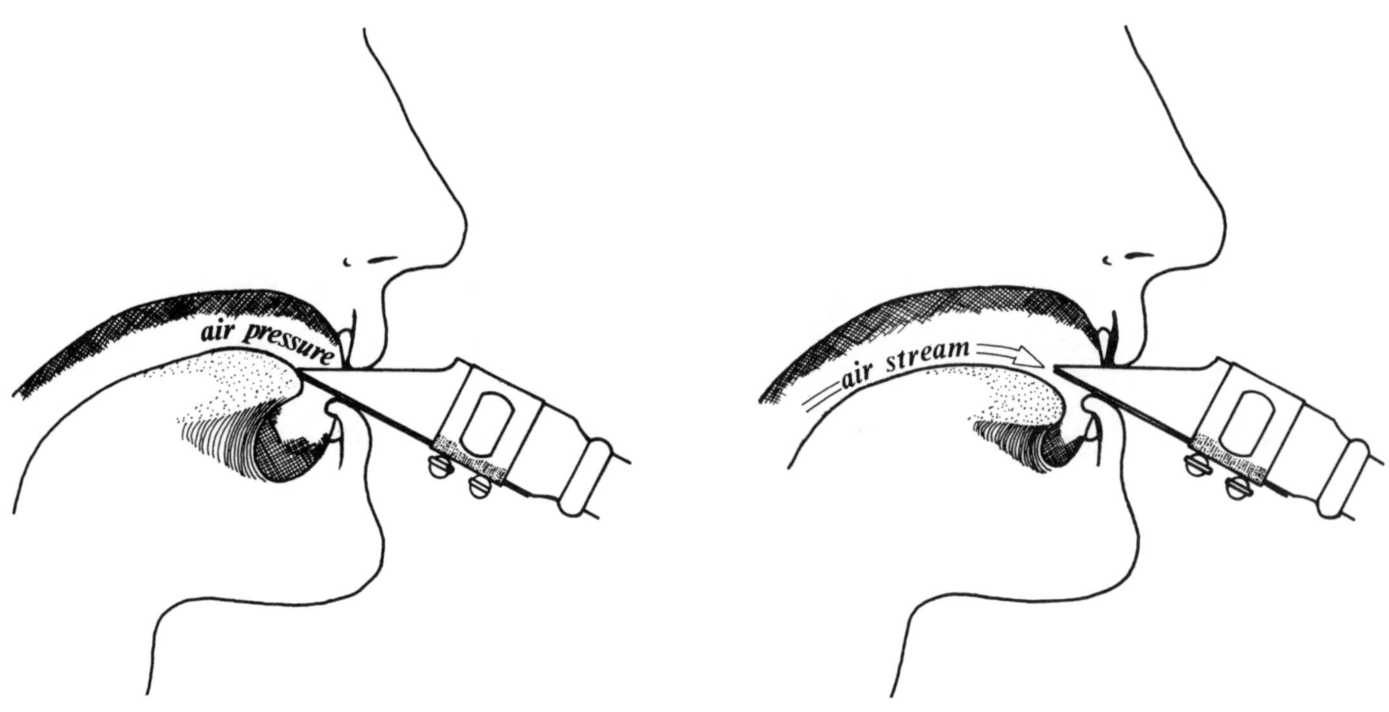


Figure 1                                                        Figure 2

# MUSICAL ARTICULATION ON THE MOUTHPIECE-NECK ASSEMBLY

**Step 1:** Inhale a full breath of air through your mouth.

> *Caution: Inhaling through your nose will prevent you from taking a full breath of air.*

**Step 2:** Form the embouchure.

**Step 3:** Demonstrate the separated style of articulation with the syllable "tu." (CD Track 3)

**Step 4:** Demonstrate the connected style of articulation with the syllable "du." (CD Track 4)

> *Caution: Movement of your lower jaw while tonguing will prevent you from producing a steady and smooth articulation.*

**CD Track 3**   *MUSICAL ARTICULATION - JUST LISTEN*

### THE SEPARATED STYLE OF ARTICULATION

**CD Track 4**   *LISTEN TO THE CD and PLAY*

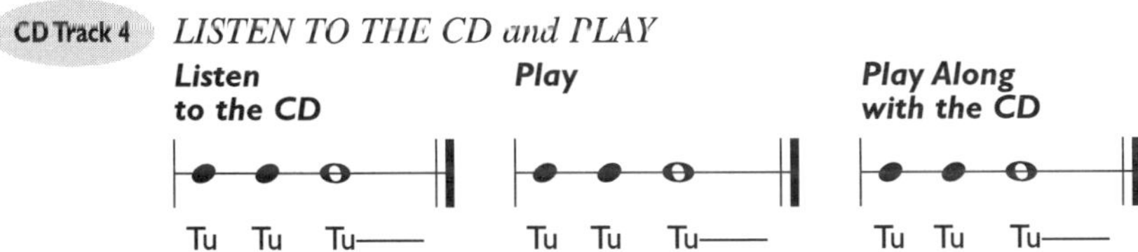


### THE CONNECTED STYLE OF ARTICULATION

**CD Track 5**   *LISTEN TO THE CD and PLAY*

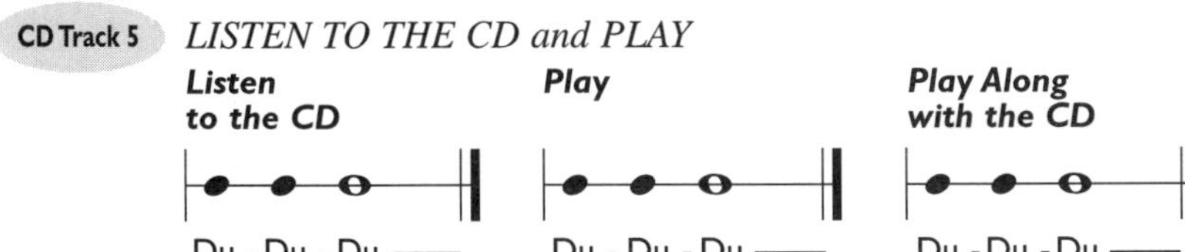


| Step | 1 | 2 | 3 | 4 |
|---|---|---|---|---|
| | 5 | 6 | 7 | 8 |
| 1 | | | | |
| 2 | | | | |
| 3 | | | | |
| 4 | | | | |

MARK ✔ or ? HERE   Week

# FOCUS ON TEACHING

## It "Sounds Right" But It Doesn't "Look Right"

- Owing to the wide range of physical characteristics among instrumental students, it may not be possible to achieve the "right look" in every case.

- "Sounds right" should overrule "looks right" unless an unusual physical set-up has the potential to compromise the long-term development of range and endurance.

## SAXOPHONE ASSEMBLY - STEP-BY-STEP

**Step 1:** Grasp the saxophone carefully by the bell and lift it out of the case.

**Step 2:** Remove the end plug from the body of your saxophone.

**Step 3:** Loosen the neck screw.

**Step 4:** Gently insert the neck into the body with a back-and-forth motion.

| MARK ✔ or ? HERE Week | | | |
|---|---|---|---|
| **Step** 1 2 3 4 | | | |
| 5 6 7 8 | | | |
| 1 | | | |
| 2 | | | |
| 3 | | | |
| 4 | | | |
| 5 | | | |

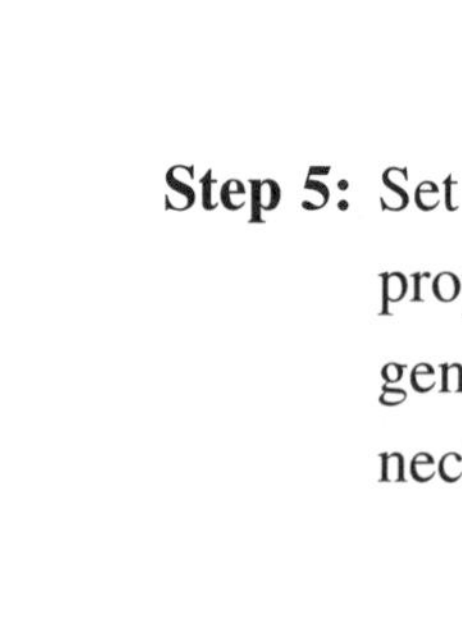

**Step 5:** Set the neck at the proper angle and gently tighten the neck screw.

**Step 6:** Hook the neck strap onto the saxophone.

*Caution: A saxophone hanging freely by the neck strap is an accident waiting to happen. Always support your saxophone with the neck strap and at least one hand.*

**Step 7:** Check the alignment of the neck and mouthpiece and adjust, if necessary.

| 6 | | | | |
|---|---|---|---|---|

| 7 | | | | |
|---|---|---|---|---|

# POSTURE AND INSTRUMENT POSITION

**Step 1:** Position your body forward on the front edge of the chair.

**Step 2:** Keep your back straight.

**Step 3:** Keep your chin up, your head erect, and your shoulders and neck muscles relaxed.

**Step 4:** Adjust the neck strap, neck, and mouthpiece so that the saxophone conforms to the position of your body.

**Step 5:** Support the entire weight of the instrument with the neck strap.

**Step 6:** Balance the instrument with your right thumb.

**Step 7:** Keep your elbows comfortably away from your body.

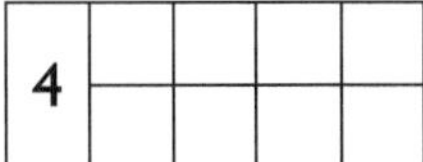

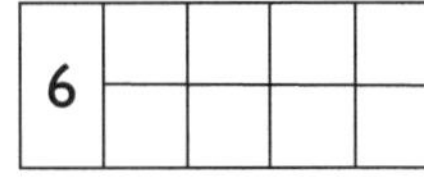
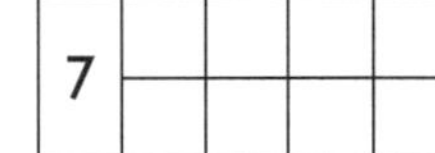

| Step | MARK ✔ or ? HERE Week | | | |
|---|---|---|---|---|
| | 1 | 2 | 3 | 4 |
| | 5 | 6 | 7 | 8 |
| 1 | | | | |
| 2 | | | | |
| 3 | | | | |
| 4 | | | | |
| 5 | | | | |
| 6 | | | | |
| 7 | | | | |

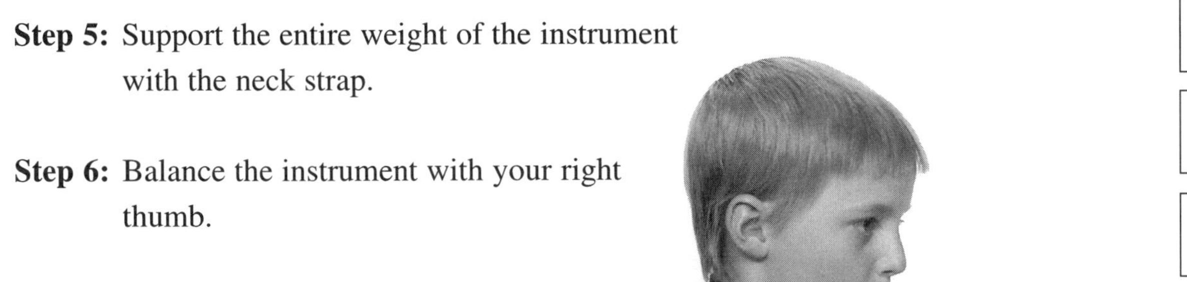

# LEFT HAND POSITION

LEFT HAND POSITION:

**Step 1:** Position your left hand to the top of the instrument.

**Step 2:** Position your left thumb on the thumb rest.

**Step 3:** Keep your fingers curved.

**Step 4:** Keep your thumb straight.

**MARK ✔ or ? HERE**

| Step | Week | | | |
|---|---|---|---|---|
| | 1 | 2 | 3 | 4 |
| | 5 | 6 | 7 | 8 |
| 1 | | | | |
| 2 | | | | |
| 3 | | | | |
| 4 | | | | |

# RIGHT HAND POSITION

RIGHT HAND POSITION:

**Step 1:** Position your right hand to the bottom of the instrument.

**Step 2:** Center your right thumb on the thumb rest between the tip of your thumb and your first knuckle.

**Step 3:** Keep your fingers curved.

**Step 4:** Keep your thumb straight.

**Step 5:** Slant your fingers comfortably upward.

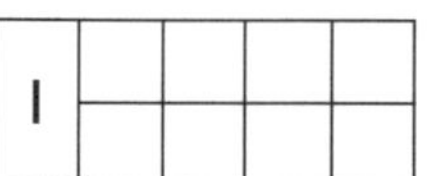
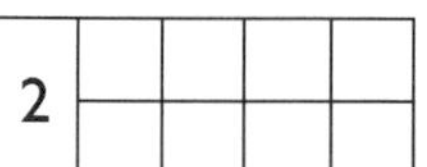

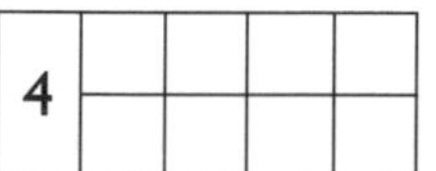

| | | | | |
|---|---|---|---|---|
| 1 | | | | |
| 2 | | | | |
| 3 | | | | |
| 4 | | | | |
| 5 | | | | |

## LEARNING TO PRODUCE A TONE ON THE ALTO SAXOPHONE

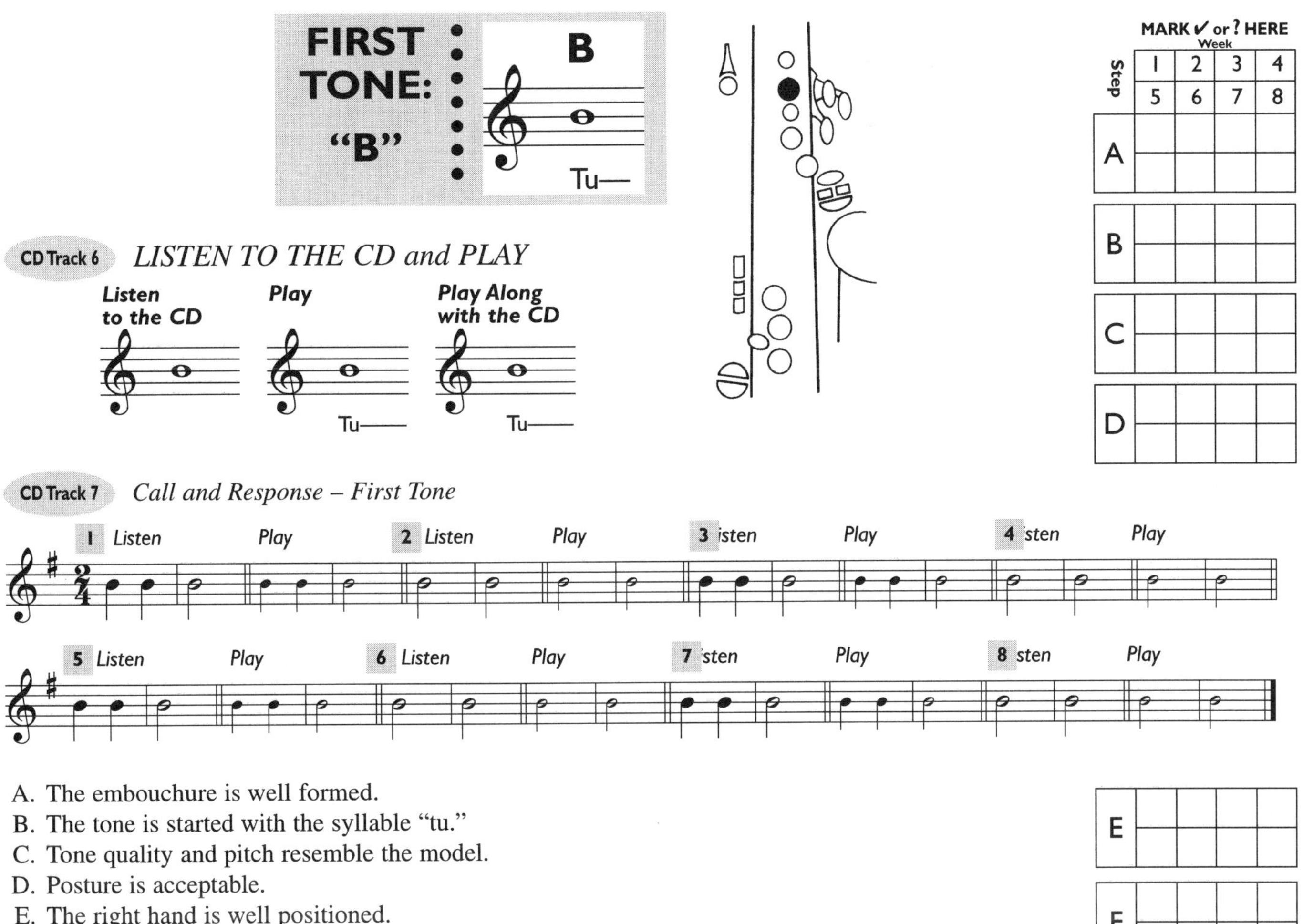


A. The embouchure is well formed.
B. The tone is started with the syllable "tu."
C. Tone quality and pitch resemble the model.
D. Posture is acceptable.
E. The right hand is well positioned.
F. The left hand is well positioned.

# FOCUS ON TEACHING MUSIC PERFORMANCE
## Telling Isn't Teaching

- To teach music performance is to show.

  "I will show you what I want you to learn."

Suggestion: Use live demonstrations, visual media, and recordings to show students what is to be learned.

## Asking Isn't Assessing

- To have learned to perform is to be able to show.

  "Show me what you have learned."

Suggestion: Use student performances to assess music playing skills and music reading.

## LEARNING TO PRODUCE ANOTHER TONE ON THE ALTO SAXOPHONE

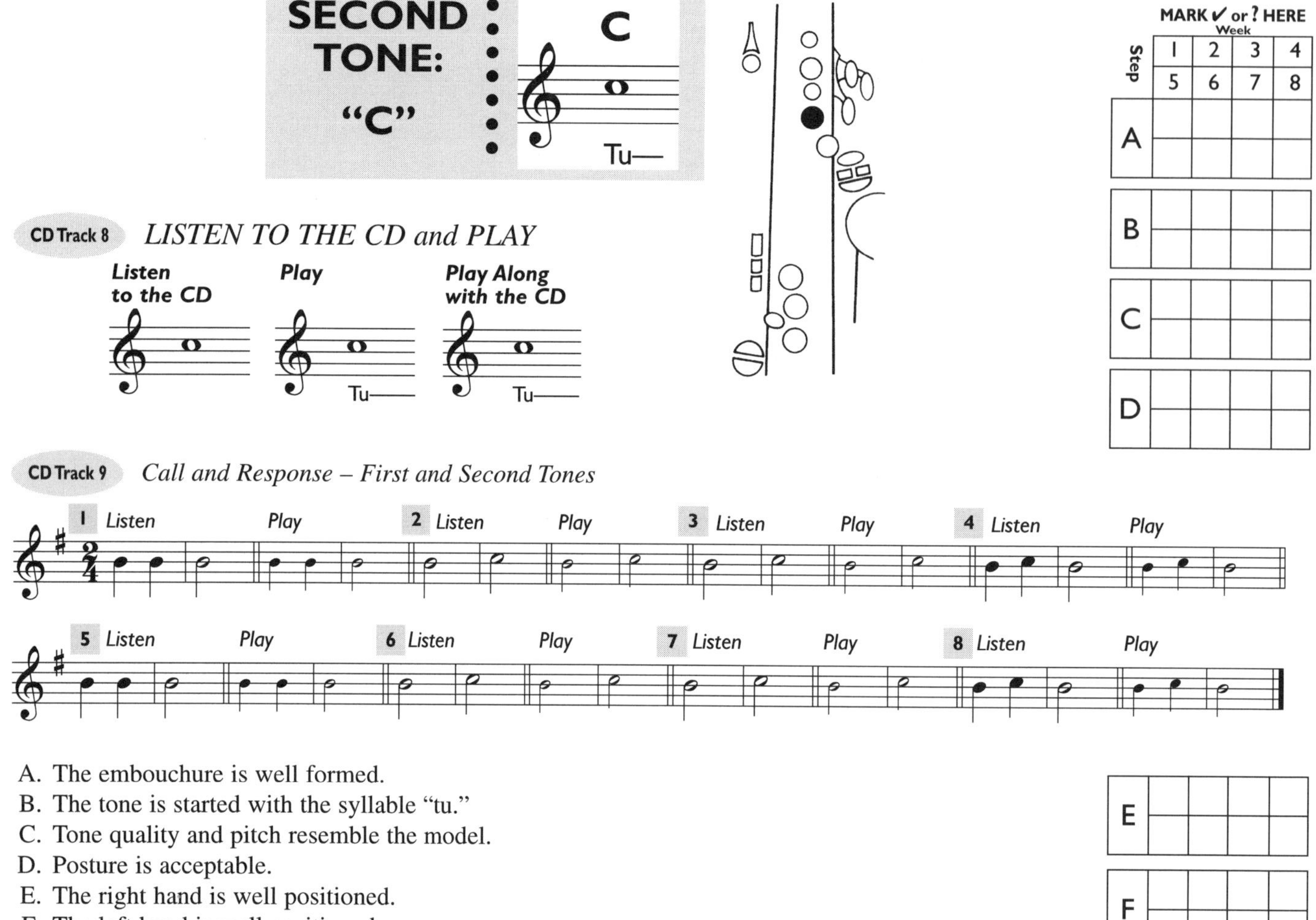



A. The embouchure is well formed.
B. The tone is started with the syllable "tu."
C. Tone quality and pitch resemble the model.
D. Posture is acceptable.
E. The right hand is well positioned.
F. The left hand is well positioned.

# FOCUS ON TEACHING

## Nonverbal Instruction versus Verbal Instruction

- A nonverbal teacher initiative uses actions rather than words to produce an intended result.

   Example: The teacher engages students in a call and response to illustrate the difference between separated and connected styles of articulation.

   Note: Nonverbal teaching saves time.

   Note: Students prefer nonverbal teaching over verbal teaching.

- A verbal teacher initiative uses words rather than actions to produce an intended result.

   Example: The teacher describes the difference between separated and connected styles of articulation.

   Note: Verbal teaching in the absence of a nonverbal model is often ineffective.

   Notable Exception: The verbal analogy can often be an effective means to connect common experience with an important musical concept.

   Example: One player with faulty intonation in a group of thirty creates a similar amount of distortion that one cloudy pane of glass creates in a row of thirty otherwise clear panes.

## LEARNING TO PRODUCE A THIRD TONE ON THE ALTO SAXOPHONE

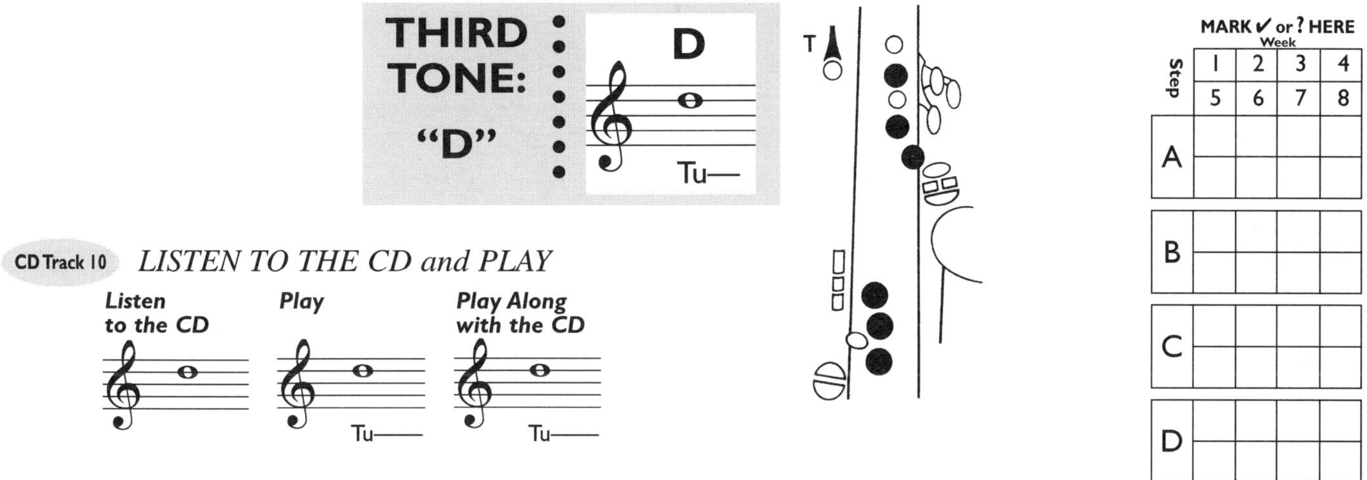


**CD Track 10**  *LISTEN TO THE CD and PLAY*

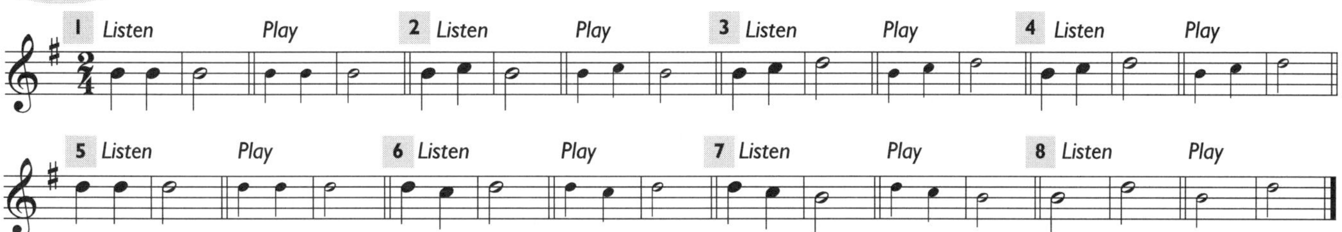


**CD Track 11**  *Call and Response – First, Second, and Third Tones*



A. The embouchure is well formed.
B. The tone is started with the syllable "tu."
C. Tone quality and pitch resemble the model.
D. Posture is acceptable.
E. The right hand is well positioned.
F. The left hand is well positioned.



# FOCUS ON TEACHING

## One-to-One in Groups of Beginning Students

- Individual Lessons to Students in a Group Is an Inefficient Use of Time.

- Individual Lessons to Students in a Group Is a Highly Problematic Teaching Strategy.
  - Non-participating students often become inattentive and bored.
  - Bored students often become disruptive.
  - Disruptive student behavior often leads to negative and oppressive teacher behavior.

Suggestion: Attend to the needs of an individual student by engaging in peer group teaching and peer group assessment to maintain group focus.

> Example: "Who can demonstrate an acceptable right hand position? .............OK!
> Now, everyone take turns checking your stand partner's right hand position."

- Recorded Call and Response Tracks Provide a Means for the Teacher to Teach One-to-One.
  - The call and response is a highly effective and efficient group music learning strategy.
  - While all students are engaged in the call and response, the teacher is free to move about the class and attend to individual students who need instruction.

Suggestion: Use CD call and response tracks at the start of class to warm-up and to assess students one-to-one.

## FIRST TUNE

### Preparation to Play *Practice Every Day March*

**CD Track 12** *Listen and Play*

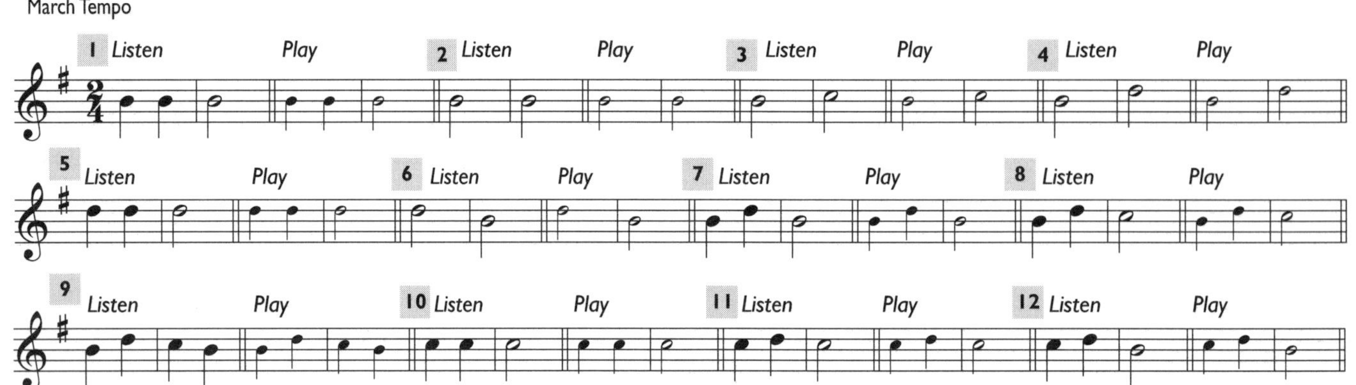


### Practice Every Day March

**CD Track 1** *1. Listen*  *2. Listen and Play Along*  **CD Track 13** *Play*

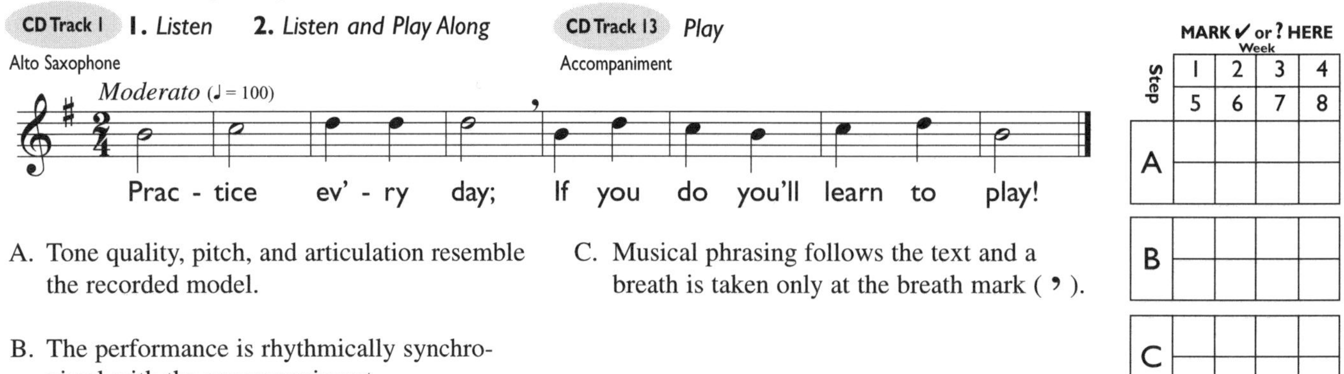


A. Tone quality, pitch, and articulation resemble the recorded model.

B. The performance is rhythmically synchronized with the accompaniment.

C. Musical phrasing follows the text and a breath is taken only at the breath mark ( ' ).

| Step | | | MARK ✔ or ? HERE Week | |
|---|---|---|---|---|

| Step | 1 | 2 | 3 | 4 |
|---|---|---|---|---|
| A | 5 | 6 | 7 | 8 |
| B | | | | |
| C | | | | |

## FOCUS ON TEACHING

## Teach Patterns

- Music is composed of patterns.

- Patterns give meaning to music.

  Note: Individual notes are to music what individual letters are to language - neither conveys much until they are grouped into meaningful patterns.

- Melodic patterns are the building blocks of musical phrases and musical form.

- Finger patterns are the building blocks of instrumental music performance.

Suggestion: Use teacher modeled or recorded call and response sequences to build pattern technique.

Suggestion: Employ rhythmic pattern flashcards and melodic pattern flashcards to teach pattern reading skills. *Band Home Helper* and *Do It! Play in Band.* www.giamusic.com

## COMPOSITE ACHIEVEMENT CHECKLIST

✔ **If Satisfactory**      ? **If More Work Is Needed**

A. Posture

B. Instrument Position

C. Left Hand Position

D. Right Hand Position

E. Embouchure

F. Musical Phrasing

G. Musical Articulation

H. Tone Quality

# FOCUS ON TEACHING

## The Keys to Effective Student Home Practice: Predicting, Discriminating, and Self-Remediation

- It is the teacher's responsibility to teach students to:

**Predict**, visually and aurally, specific objectives for practice.

"It Looks Like" - "It Sounds Like"

**Discriminate** the differences between visual and aural practice objectives and existing performance discrepancies.

"It Looks Like This" - "It Doesn't Look Like This"
"It Sounds Like This" - "It Doesn't Sound Like This"

Suggestion: Model both the performance objective and the performance discrepancy to teach students to discriminate the difference between "*What it is*" and "*What it isn't.*"

**Remediate** performance problems with effective practice strategies.

"Use a mirror to look and compare."
"Use your CD player to listen and compare."
"Record performances to listen and compare."

Note: Effective home practice requires the same skills teachers need to teach well: the skills to predict, discriminate, and remediate.

# FOCUS ON TEACHING

## Assessment

**Assessment of Music Achievement Requires Three Components:**
- Specific, Observable Criteria
- An Aural or Visual Model for Reference
- A Record of Achievement

**Assessment Takes Three Fundamental Forms:**
- Teacher Assessment
- Peer Assessment
- Self-Assessment

## Performance Achievement Checklist

| 1. PHYSICAL/TECHNICAL CRITERIA | EXEMPLARY | ACCEPTABLE | QUESTIONABLE | UNACCEPTABLE |
| --- | --- | --- | --- | --- |
| A. Posture | ☐ | ☐ | ☐ | ☐ |
| B. Instrument Position | ☐ | ☐ | ☐ | ☐ |
| C. Left Hand Position | ☐ | ☐ | ☐ | ☐ |
| D. Right Hand Position | ☐ | ☐ | ☐ | ☐ |
| E. Embouchure | ☐ | ☐ | ☐ | ☐ |
| F. Breathing and Breath Control | ☐ | ☐ | ☐ | ☐ |

| 2. MUSICAL CRITERIA | EXEMPLARY | ACCEPTABLE | QUESTIONABLE | UNACCEPTABLE |
| --- | --- | --- | --- | --- |
| A. Tone Quality | ☐ | ☐ | ☐ | ☐ |
| B. Intonation | ☐ | ☐ | ☐ | ☐ |
| C. Articulation (Separated) | ☐ | ☐ | ☐ | ☐ |
| D. Articulation (Connected) | ☐ | ☐ | ☐ | ☐ |
| E. Musical Phrasing | ☐ | ☐ | ☐ | ☐ |
| F. Expressive Nuance | ☐ | ☐ | ☐ | ☐ |

Suggestion: Use this "Permission to Copy" form to engage in Teacher Assessment, Peer Assessment, and Self-Assessment.

# FOCUS ON TEACHING

## "Sound" Teaching – The Achievement Loop

1. A "SOUND" MUSIC LEARNING OBJECTIVE

   The achievement loop starts with recorded music repertoire that is contained on the CD, performed by an artist, and set in an authentic music context that defines:

   - Tempo
   - Rhythm
   - Pitch
   - Melody
   - Phrasing
   - Tone Quality
   - Harmony
   - Expressive Nuance
   - Form

   A "sound" concept of the music learning objective motivates students for:

2. PREPARATION
   The teacher prepares the students for:

3. PRACTICE
   Practice leads to:

4. ACHIEVEMENT
   Student achievement pleases everyone and motivates the student to pursue:

5. A NEW "SOUND" MUSIC LEARNING OBJECTIVE
   A new achievement loop (1. above) starts with recorded music repertoire contained on the CD, performed by an artist, and set in an authentic music context.

# FOCUS ON TEACHING

## The Conditions for Learning[1]

In any classroom, the following conditions are necessary for efficient learning:

1. clearly delineated learning tasks
2. a stable environment
3. opportunity for self-selection of tasks
4. opportunity for independent work
5. closure and feedback (on achievement and behavior)

---

[1] Judith M. Smith and Donald E. P. Smith, *Classroom Management* (New York, N.Y.: Learning Research Associates, Inc., 1980).

# FOCUS ON TEACHING

## Singing – A Primary Tool for Teaching and Assessing

- Singing Develops Important Musical Skills.
- Singing Develops Concepts that Guide Home Practice.
- Singing Provides a Means to Assess Fundamental Musicianship.

Note: Students sing about as well as they hear.

Suggestion 1: Always sing to recorded models or accompaniments.

Suggestion 2: Accompany singing with rhythmic movement such as a lap-pat or heel-tap.

*BALLAD* – *A short, simple song in a narrative or descriptive style*

# FOCUS ON TEACHING

## Rhythmic Movement - A Primary Tool for Teaching and Assessing

- Rhythm is the organizing principle of music performance.

  - Rhythm is what makes music move.
  - Rhythm is what holds music together.

- The ability to synchronize rhythmic movement to music is an important prerequisite to the development of music listening, reading, writing, and performance skills. Moving well to music is also an aesthetic experience.

  - We learn rhythm best by listening and moving.

Suggestion: Use synchronous rhythmic movement to music to demonstrate steady beat for students.[1]  Examples of synchronous rhythmic movement include heel-taps, lap-pats, toe-taps, finger-snaps, and hand-claps.

- Movement to music provides a means to assess rhythmic musicianship. One element of rhythmic musicianship is the ability to synchronize movement to the primary beat of music.

  - The primary beat of music is best defined by the ictus of the conductor's baton.

Suggestion: To assess students' understanding of the primary beat in music, direct them to close their eyes, listen to the music, and lap-pat the primary beat in time with the music.

[1] Refer to *Movement to Music in Confined Spaces* (Weikart and Froseth, MLR-188); *Music For Movement* (Blaser and Froseth, MLR 187CD); and *Move to the Sound of World Music* (Froseth, CD-668). www.giamusic.com

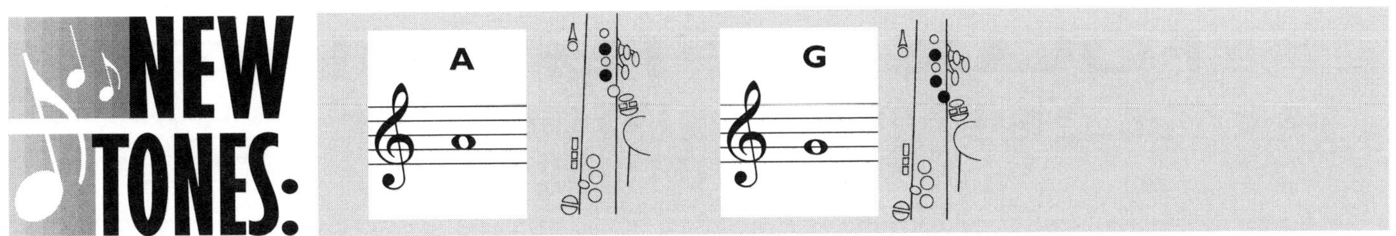


**FOLK SONG** – *A song reflecting the traditions of the people of a country or region and forming part of their characteristic culture.*

Model Tr. 17
Accom. Tr. 17-1

**1. Hot Cross Buns**

English Folk Song

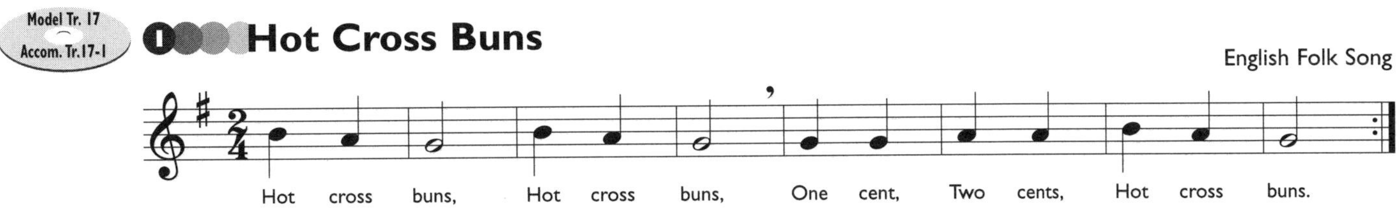


**BLUEGRASS** – *A type of Anglo-American folk music originating around the mid-1940s in rural Appalachia.*

Model Tr. 18
Accom. Tr. 18-1

**2. Mary Had A Little Lamb**

Traditional Folk Song

Model Tr. 19
Accom. Tr. 19-1

**3. Au Claire de la Lune**

French Folk Song

**LULLABY** – *A cradle song, usually sung by a mother to soothe or quiet an infant before bedtime.*

Model Tr. 20
Accom. Tr. 20-1

**4. Fais do do**

French Lullaby

# FOCUS ON TEACHING
## Learning What Something "Is Not" Can Help Teach What Something "Is"

- Major Tonality Is Not Minor Tonality
- Minor Tonality Is Not Major Tonality

Suggestion: Use CD models to contrast the different sounds of major tonality and minor tonality.

**TONALITY** – *A characteristic of Western music referring to the relationship of pitches to a specific tonal center. If Do is the tonal center, the tonality is Major. If La is the tonal center, the tonality is Minor.*

Model Tr. 21 / Accom. Tr. 21-1

**❶ Au Claire de la Lune** (IN MINOR TONALITY)

French Folk Song

Model Tr. 22 / Accom. Tr. 22-1

**❷ Fais do do** (IN MINOR TONALITY)

French Lullaby

# FOCUS ON TEACHING
## Musical Independence

- Musical Rounds Help to Develop Musical Independence
- Musical Rounds Prepare Students for Ensemble Performance

Suggestion: Allow students to determine when to enter the round without help.

**ROUND** – *A specially composed melody that allows two or more individuals to create interesting musical effects by starting the melody at different times.*

**❸ Lady My** (2-PART ROUND)

English Round

**❹ Be-A-Round** (4-PART ROUND)

U. S.

# FOCUS ON TEACHING
## The Power of Music Modeling

**Recorded and Live Music Models Serve to:**

- Define Performance Objectives

- Exemplify Performance Objectives

- Motivate Students to Practice and Play

Suggestion: Always listen first to the recorded artist model on your CD before you begin to practice. A well developed concept of the objective is essential to guide one to the desired outcome.

# FOCUS ON TEACHING
## Musical Context

**Recorded Accompaniments Provide Musical Context that Informs Students about:**

- Tempo
- Rhythm
- Intonation
- Melody
- Tone Quality
- Timbre
- Harmony
- Form
- Expressive Nuance
- Musical Style

Suggestion: Practice until you are able to play along with the model and accompaniment tracks on your CD.

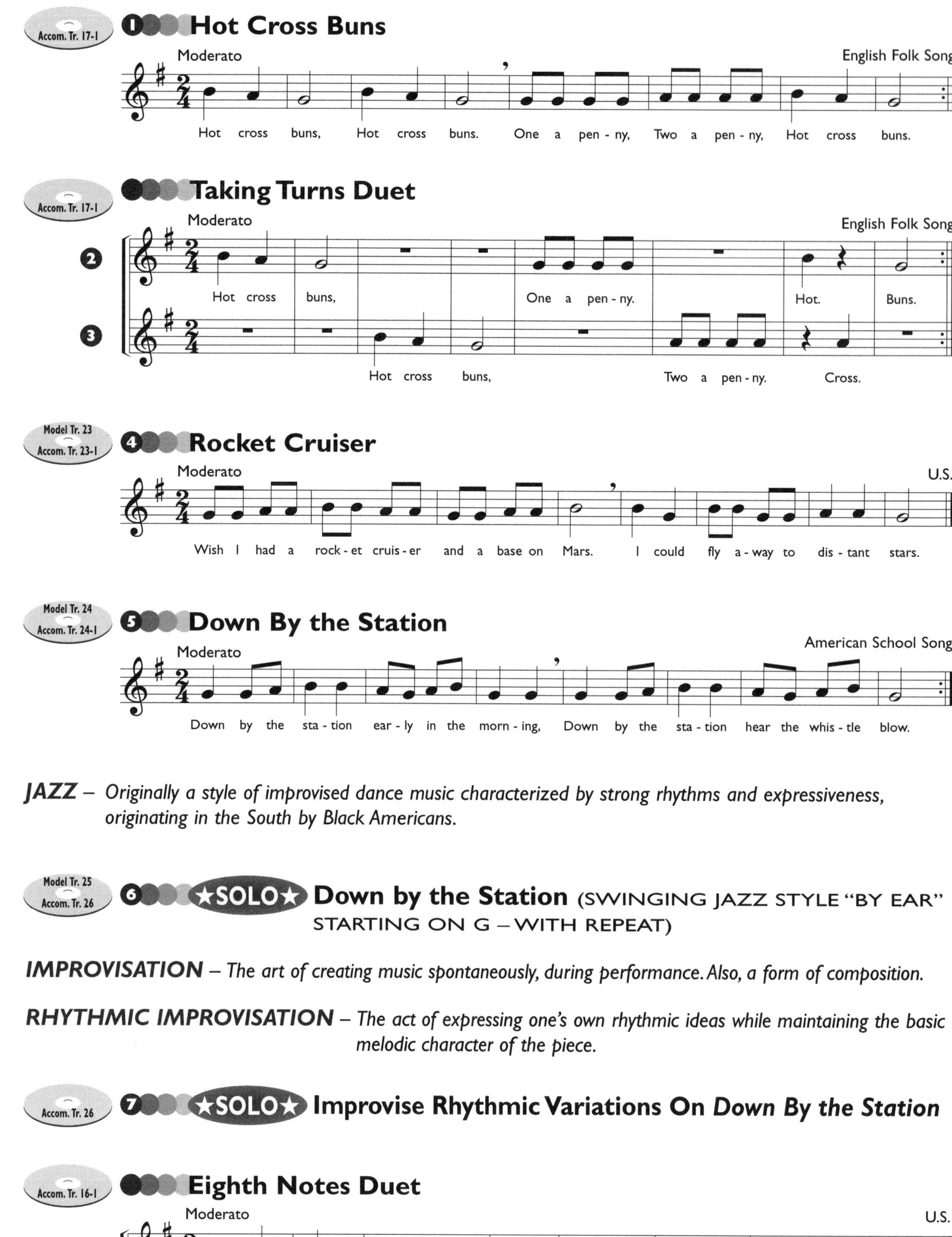


**JAZZ** – *Originally a style of improvised dance music characterized by strong rhythms and expressiveness, originating in the South by Black Americans.*



**6 ★SOLO★ Down by the Station** (SWINGING JAZZ STYLE "BY EAR" STARTING ON G – WITH REPEAT)

**IMPROVISATION** – *The art of creating music spontaneously, during performance. Also, a form of composition.*

**RHYTHMIC IMPROVISATION** – *The act of expressing one's own rhythmic ideas while maintaining the basic melodic character of the piece.*



**7 ★SOLO★ Improvise Rhythmic Variations On *Down By the Station***

# FOCUS ON TEACHING

## Creating a Safe Environment for Spontaneous Music Making

**Down By the Station** (JAZZ STYLE)

**PRINCIPLE A:** KEEP IT SIMPLE (Too many options can inhibit creativity)

    **PROCEDURE 1:** Direct students to "Use the tones Concert B♭, C, and D"

**PRINCIPLE B:** KEEP EVERYONE INVOLVED (Peer observation can be intimidating)

    **PROCEDURE 2:** Teach everyone an 8-beat riff (melodic ostinato)
    *(NOTE: Riffs may be improvised and taught to the class by the teacher or by students)*

Example (As notated)

Example (As performed in a swinging style ²₄ ♩♩ = ⁶₈ ♩ ♪ )

    **PROCEDURE 3:** Direct students to "Repeat the riff until the music ends"

**PRINCIPLE C:** ALLOW FOR SELF-SELECTION OF TASKS *(A strategy designed to avoid the no–play freeze)*

    **PROCEDURE 4:** When individual students are chosen or volunteer, suggest that they:

    **A.** "Play the riff"

    **B.** "Improvise rhythmic variations on the riff, or"

    **C.** "Improvise rhythmic/melodic variations on the riff"

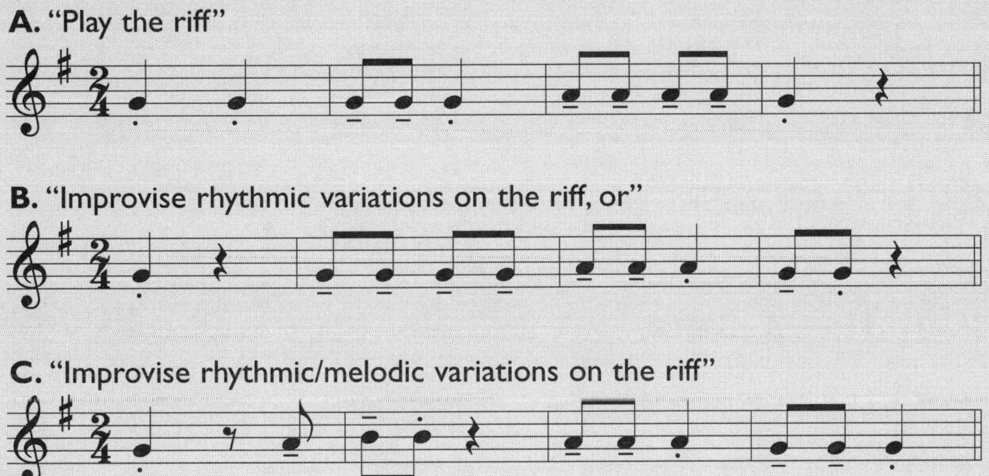

**PRINCIPLE D:** AVOID COMMON CREATIVITY KILLERS INCLUDING EXPRESSIONS OF APPROVAL OR DISAPPROVAL, SURVEILLANCE, EVALUATION, REWARD SYSTEMS, AND COMPETITION

# FOCUS ON TEACHING

## Summary of Strategies for Creating Music Improvisations That Are Interesting and Well-Structured

### Down By the Station (JAZZ STYLE)

**The Tune:** Down By the Station (in a swinging style)

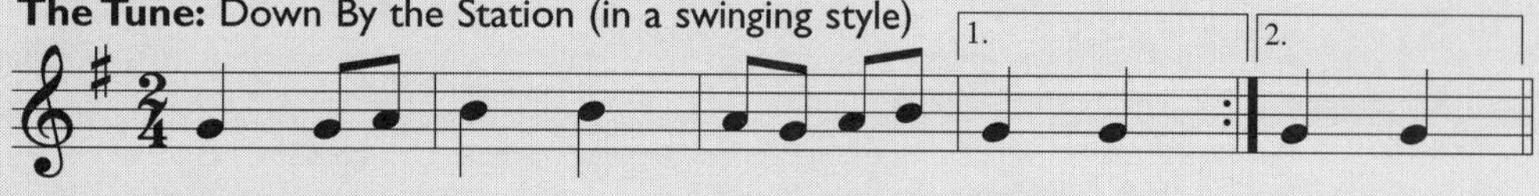

**1.** Example of the use of *Rhythmic Subdivision* as an energizing strategy

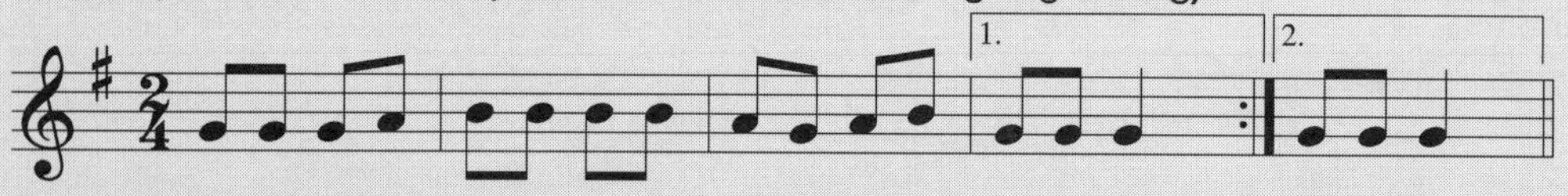

**2.** Example of the use of *Sound and Silence* as an expressive strategy and structural element

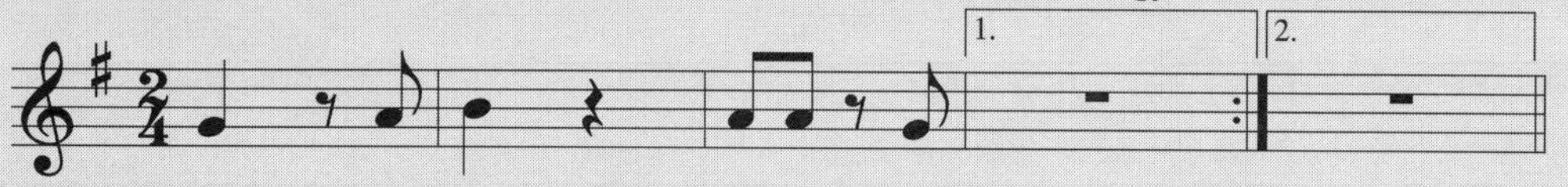

**3.** Example of the use of *Repetition (Rhythmic)* and *Variation (Melodic)* as structural elements

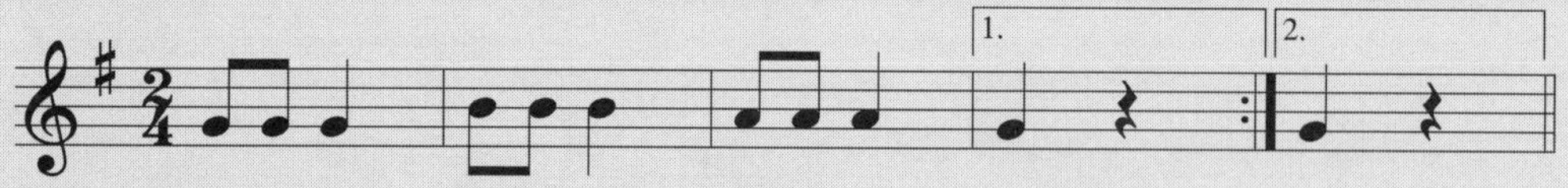

**4.** Example of the use of *Repetition (Rhythmic)* and *Variation (Melodic)* as structural elements

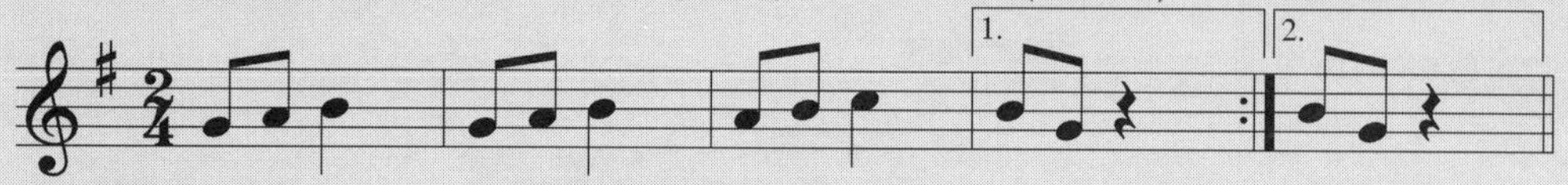

**5.** Example of the use of *Musical Articulation* as an expressive strategy

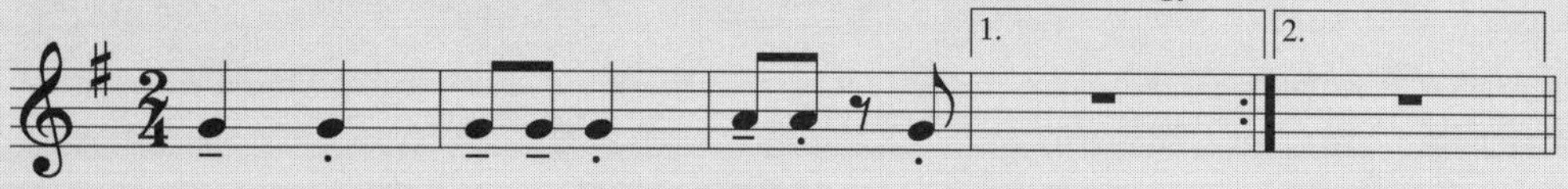

**6.** Example of the use of *Musical Dynamics* as an expressive strategy

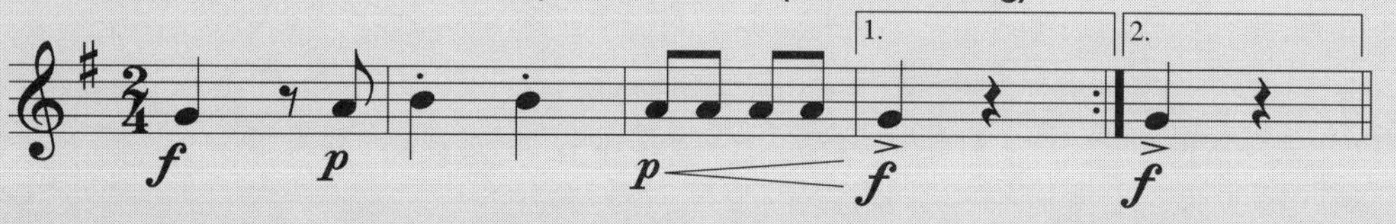

**7.** Example of the use of selected tones of the *Blues Scale* as an expressive strategy

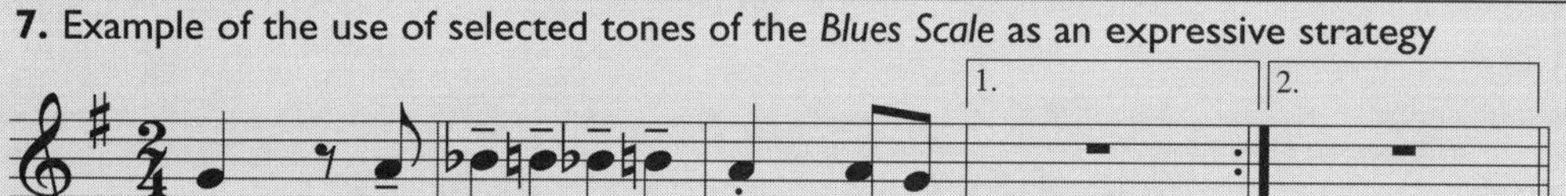

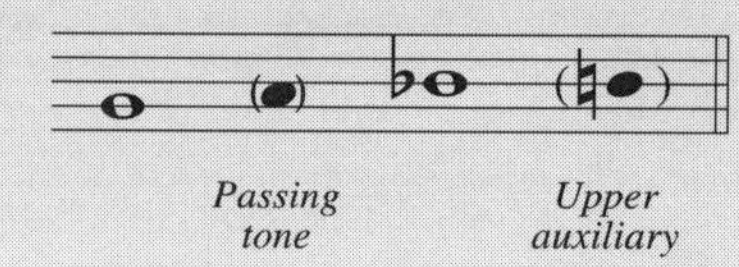

**8.** Example of the use of selected tones of the *Blues Scale* as an expressive strategy

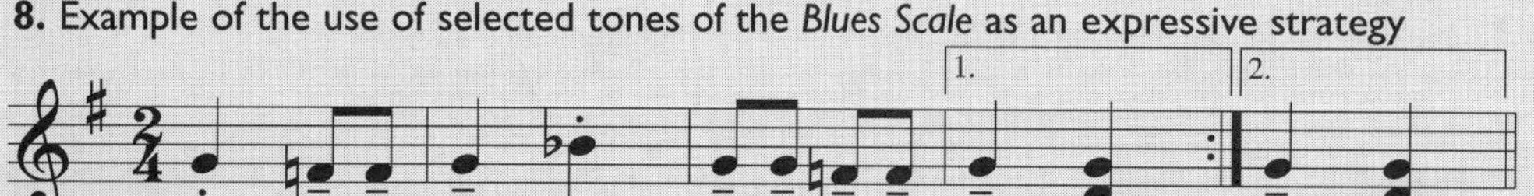

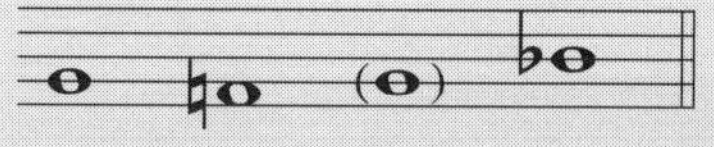

**9.** Example of the use of selected tones of the *Blues Scale* as an expressive strategy

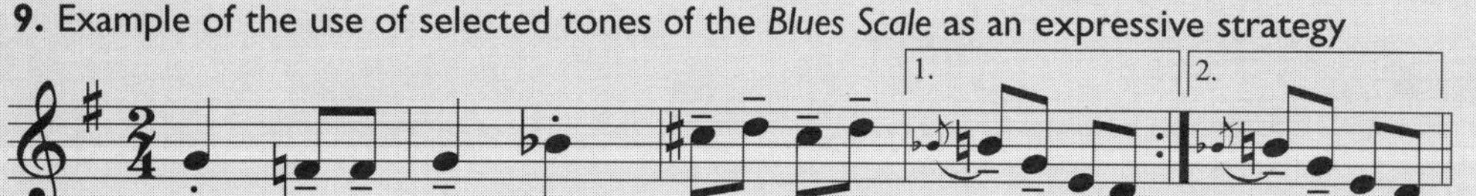

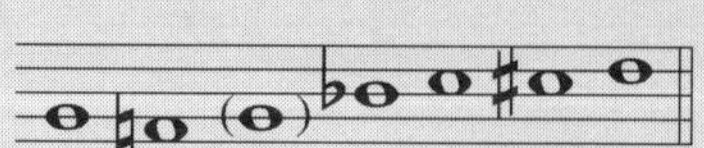

*REGGAE* – *A musical style mixing African and Caribbean rhythms often attributed to Jamaican sources.*

# FOCUS ON TEACHING
## Don't Slow It Down; Break It Down

**Step 1.** Analyze the Composition for Number of Melodic Patterns

*Cobbler, Cobbler* is composed of three different 4-beat melodic patterns

**Step 2.** Decompose Each Pattern and then Recompose Each in a Sequence that Progresses from Easier Patterns to the Composed Pattern

**Step 3.** Employ the Teacher Call/Student Response to Develop the Technique and Articulation Skills Required to Play *Cobbler, Cobbler*

**Teacher:** "The starting note of the first pattern is D"

**Suggestion:** Maintain the tempo of the CD model of *Cobbler, Cobbler*.

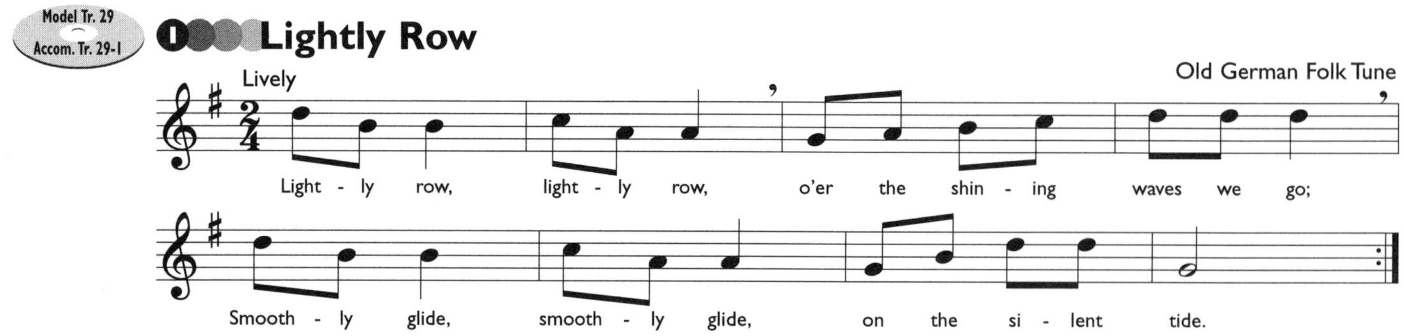


**DIXIELAND JAZZ** – *An early style of African American jazz music originating in new Orleans*

**AURAL TRANSCRIPTION** – *Learning to play recorded music "by ear" without the aid of music notation. Also, the transfer of music heard to notation.*

**2 ★SOLO★ Play *When the Saints Go Marching In* Starting On G**

# FOCUS ON TEACHING

## The Values of Learning to Play "By Ear"

- Playing "By Ear" Is an Important and Useful Musical Skill
- Playing "By Ear" Develops a Connection Between the Musical Ear and the Hand
- Playing "By Ear" Allows Students to Pursue Their Musical Interests Independently

**BLUES** – *An African American folk music characterized by spontaneity and deep emotions.*

**CALL AND RESPONSE** – *A musical alteration between two performers or a performer and a group of performers. The musical response to the call may be imitated or improvised.*

**3 ★SOLO★ Blues in F** (IMITATED RESPONSE – "BY EAR" STARTING ON D)

**4 ★SOLO★ Blues in F** (IMPROVISED RESPONSE – "BY EAR" STARTING ON ANY NOTE)

**5 ★SOLO★ Improvise Over the 12-Bar Blues in F**

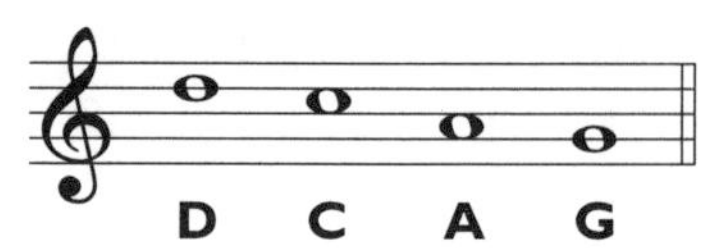


# FOCUS ON TEACHING

## The Components of a Performance-Based Listening Experience

- Listen - to focus attention on sound
- Hear - to comprehend with the ear
- Respond - to perform what is heard

Suggestion: Use aural transcription and call and response to assess how well students are listening and hearing.

***THEME AND VARIATIONS*** – *A musical form based upon a melody followed by a succession of composed rhythmic/melodic variations.*

Model Tr. 34
Accom. Tr. 34-1

**❶ Shepherd's Hey**

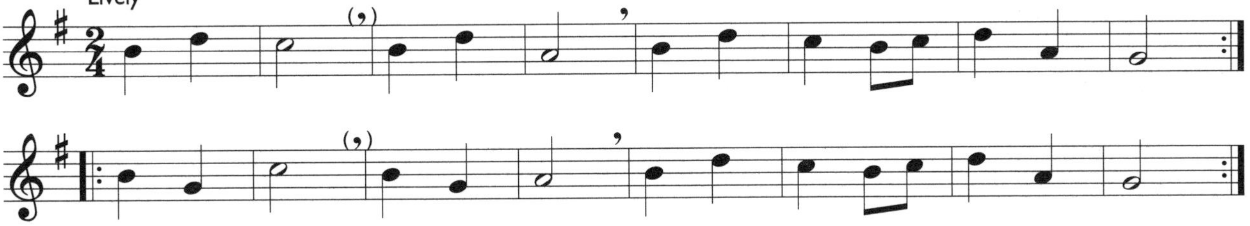

Accom. Tr. 34-1

**❷ Variation One on *Shepherd's Hey***

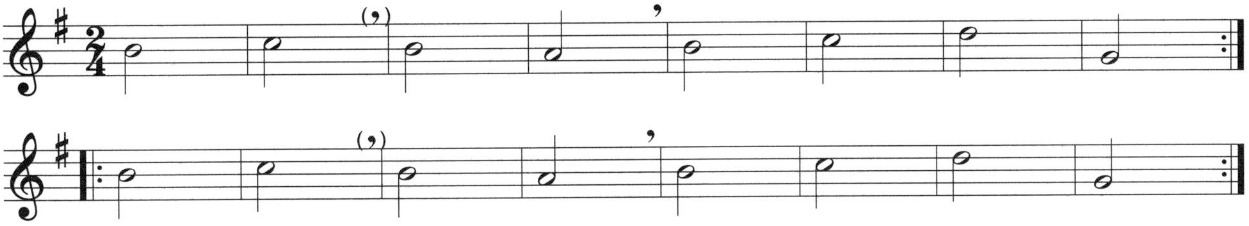

Accom. Tr. 34-1

**❸ Variation Two on *Shepherd's Hey***

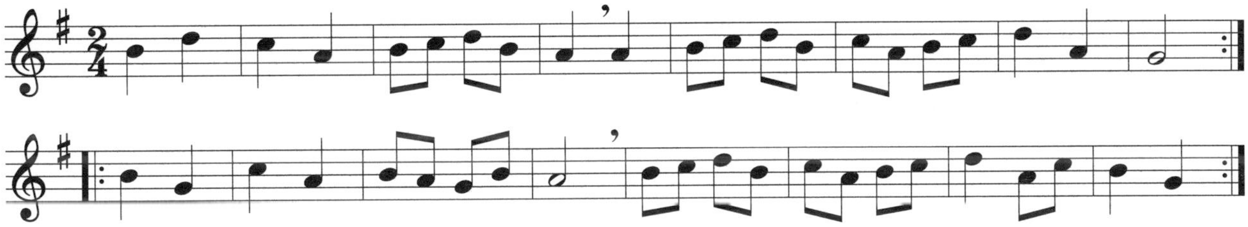

***COUNTRY MUSIC*** – *A popular style of music that originated in the American South and West.*

SPECIAL PROJECT **– Learn to Play a Song "By Ear"**

Model Tr. 35
Accom. Tr. 35-1

**❹ ★SOLO★ Play *Jingle Bells* Starting on B**

**❺ Day Is Done** (4-PART ROUND)

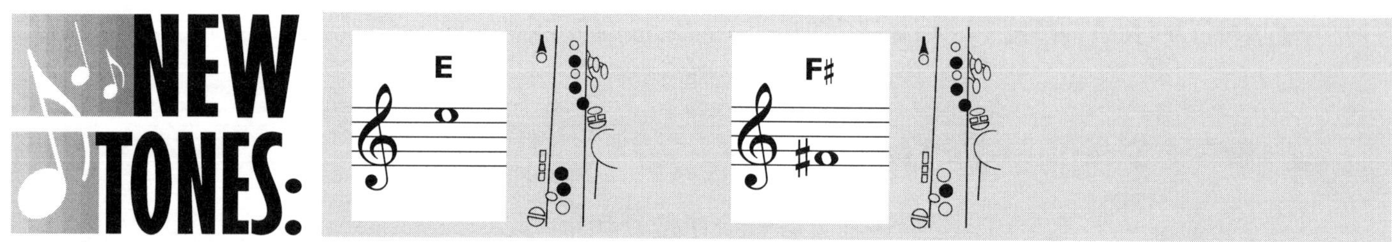


***D.C. AL FINE*** – *Go back to the beginning and end at the fine.*

Model Tr. 36
Accom. Tr. 36-1

**❶ Twinkle, Twinkle, Little Star** (SOLO, DUET, TRIO, OR QUARTET)

French Folk Tune
Text by Jane and Ann Taylor (1806)

Model Tr. 36

**❷ Harmony Part One to *Twinkle, Twinkle, Little Star***

Model Tr. 36

**❸ Harmony Part Two to *Twinkle, Twinkle, Little Star***

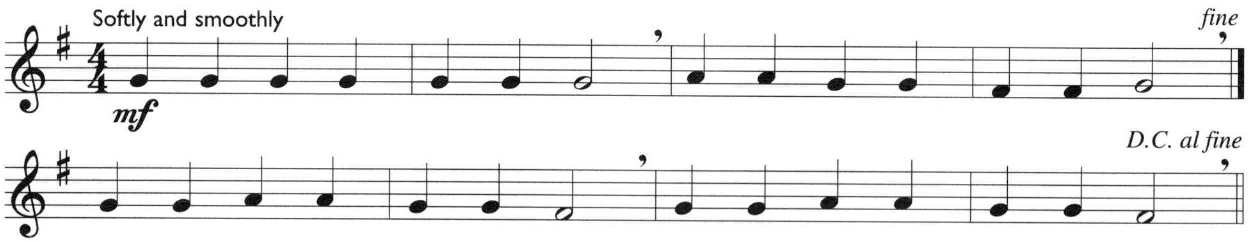


Model Tr. 36

**❹ Obbligato to *Twinkle, Twinkle, Little Star***

***SWING STYLE*** – *A type of Big Band jazz of the late 1930s and 1940s.*

Model Tr. 37
Accom. Tr. 37-1

**❺ ★SOLO★ Twinkle, Twinkle, Little Star** (SWING STYLE "BY EAR"
STARTING ON G)

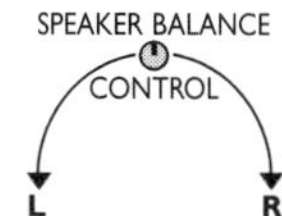


*This symbol indicates that the Left Speaker to Right speaker balance of the music can be controlled by the Speaker Balance Control Knob on your stereo. For accompaniment only, turn the Speaker Balance Control Knob to the extreme right.*

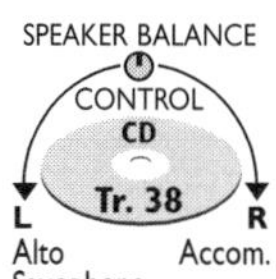


## ❶ Die Abendglocke (Evening Bells)
## Oh, How Lovely Is the Evening (3-PART ROUND)

## ❷ Cuckoo Song

## SPECIAL PROJECT – Learn to Play a Song "By Ear"

## ❸ ★SOLO★ Play *Fais do do* Starting on E

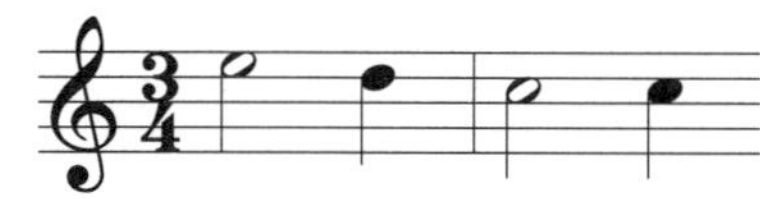

## ❹ Round Evening (4–PART ROUND)

## ❺ Round Evening Two (4–PART ROUND)

*Round Evening* and *Round Evening Two* may be played simultaneously.

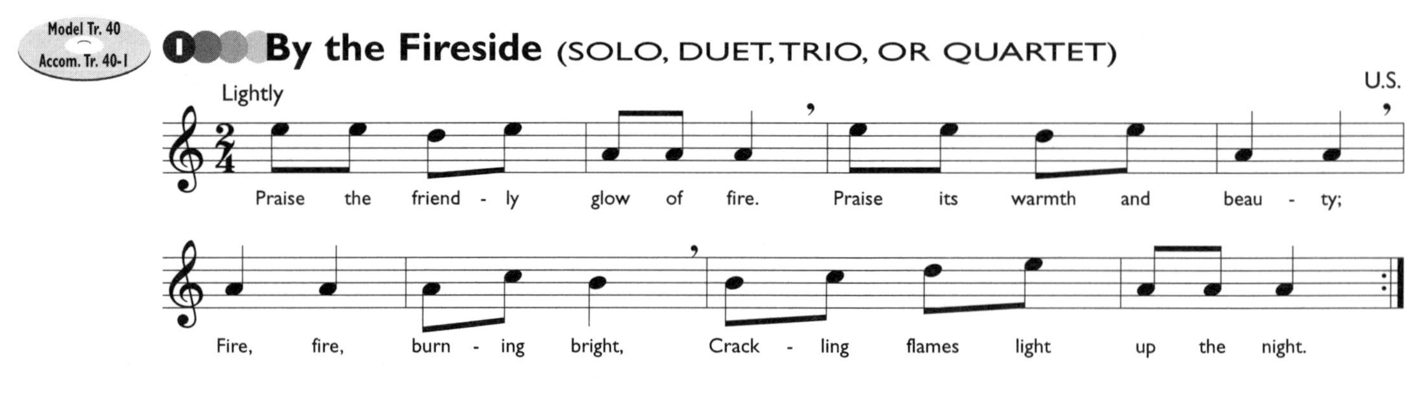

Model Tr. 40
Accom. Tr. 40-1
1 By the Fireside (SOLO, DUET, TRIO, OR QUARTET)
U.S.
Lightly
Praise the friend - ly glow of fire. Praise its warmth and beau - ty;
Fire, fire, burn - ing bright, Crack - ling flames light up the night.


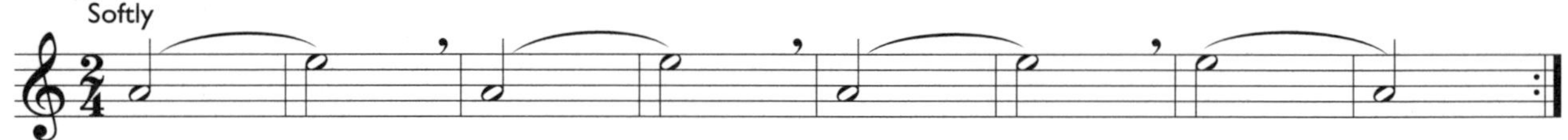

Model Tr. 40
2 Accompaniment One to By the Fireside
Softly

Model Tr. 40
3 Accompaniment Two to By the Fireside
Softly and lightly

Model Tr. 40
4 Obbligato to By the Fireside
Softly and lightly

5 Round Dance (4–PART ROUND IN MINOR TONALITY)
Lightly M.M. ♩ = 132
U.S.
1. 2. 3. 4.


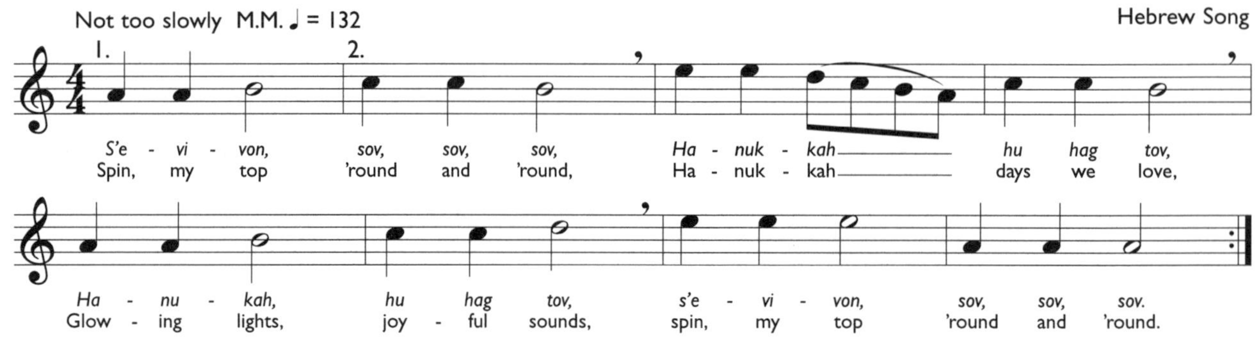

6 S'evivon Round (Spin, My Top) (2–PART ROUND)
Not too slowly M.M. ♩ = 132
Hebrew Song
1. 2.
S'e - vi - von, sov, sov, sov, Ha - nuk - kah hu hag tov,
Spin, my top 'round and 'round, Ha - nuk - kah days we love,
Ha - nu - kah, hu hag tov, s'e - vi - von, sov, sov, sov.
Glow - ing lights, joy - ful sounds, spin, my top 'round and 'round.

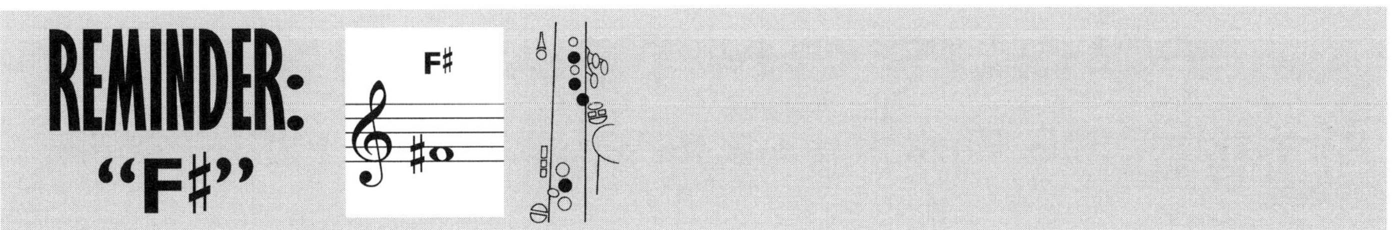


*HYMN* – *A song of worship.*

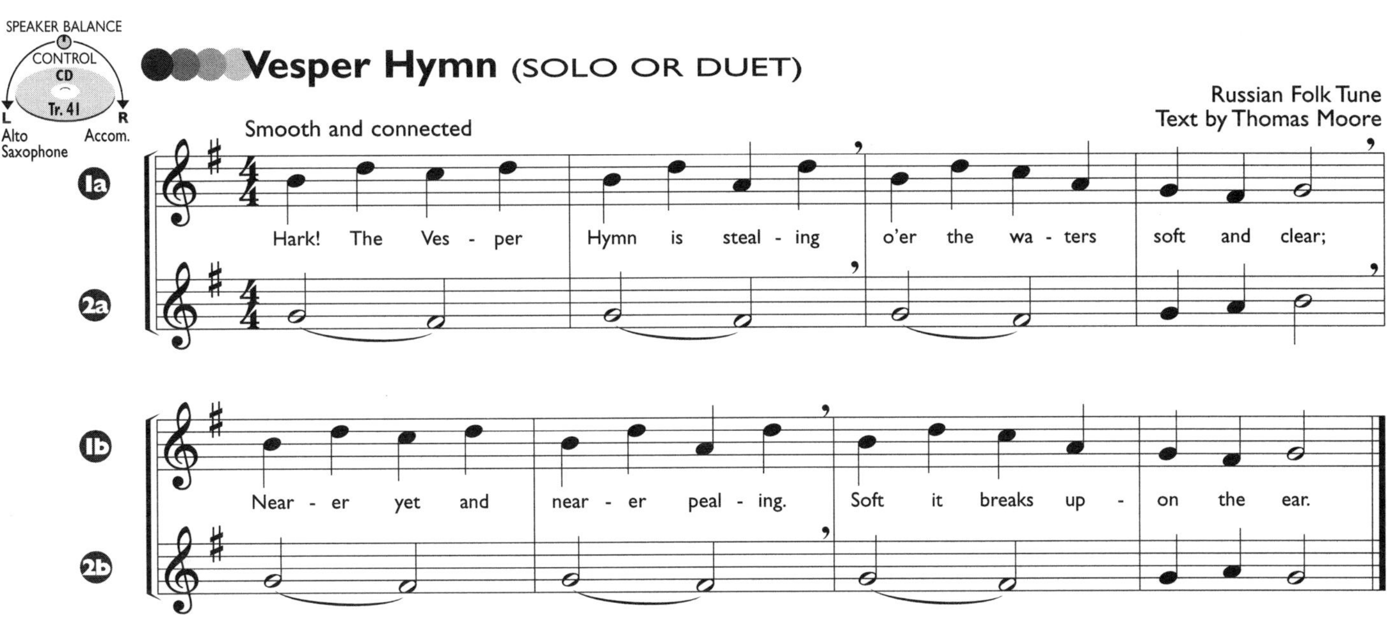


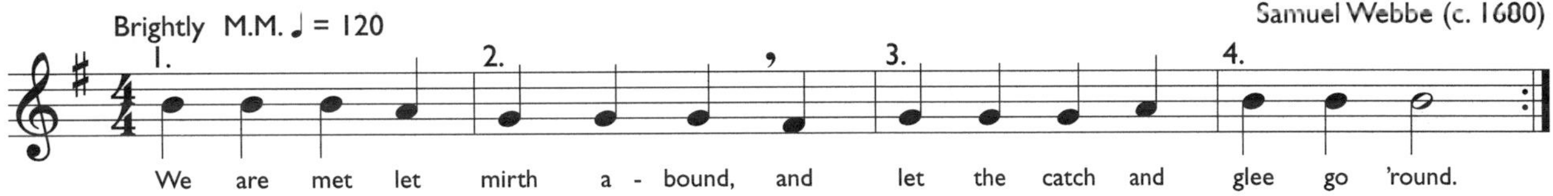

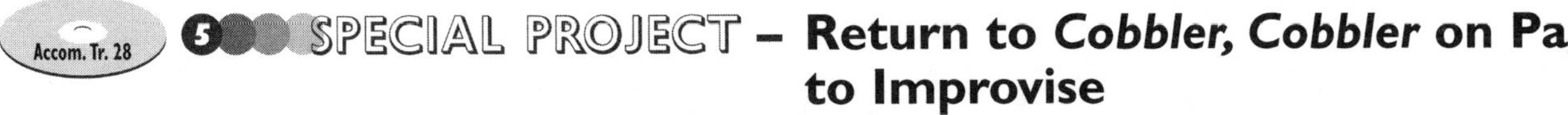


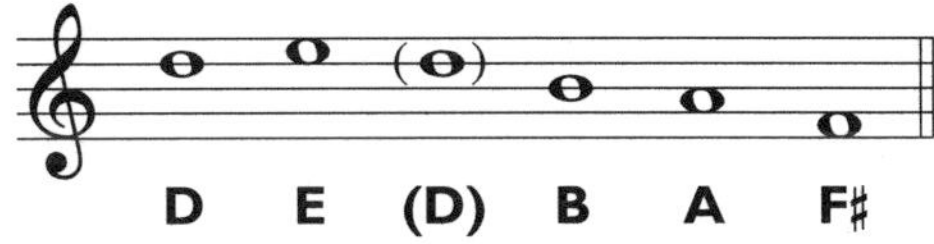

# FOCUS ON TEACHING

## Creating a Safe Environment for Spontaneous Music Making

 **Cobbler, Cobbler**

**PRINCIPLE A:** KEEP IT SIMPLE (Too many options can inhibit creativity)

**PROCEDURE 1:** Direct students to "Use the tones D, B, and A"

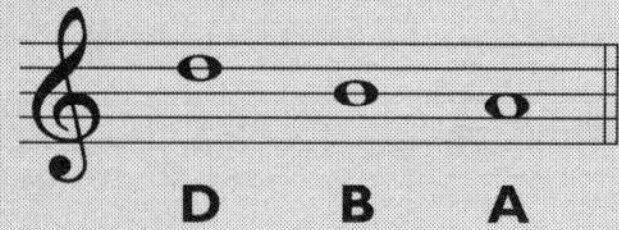


**PRINCIPLE B:** KEEP EVERYONE INVOLVED (Peer observation can be intimidating)

**PROCEDURE 2:** Teach everyone an 8-beat riff (melodic ostinato)
*(NOTE: Riffs may be improvised and taught to the class by the teacher or by students)*

**PROCEDURE 3:** Direct students to "Repeat the riff until the music ends"

**PRINCIPLE C:** ALLOW FOR SELF-SELECTION OF TASKS *(Absence of options can stifle creativity)*

**PROCEDURE 4:** When individual students are chosen or volunteer, suggest that they:

**A.** "Play the riff"

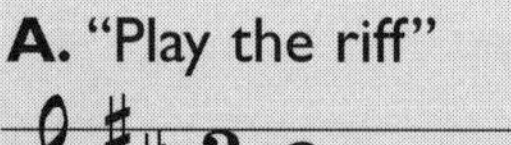

**B.** "Improvise rhythmic variations on the riff"

**C.** "Improvise melodic/rhythmic variations on the riff"

**PRINCIPLE D:** AVOID COMMON CREATIVITY KILLERS INCLUDING EXPRESSIONS OF APPROVAL OR DISAPPROVAL, SURVEILLANCE, EVALUATION, REWARD SYSTEMS, AND COMPETITION

# FOCUS ON TEACHING
## Developing and Assessing Musical Independence

- Multi-Level Musical Rounds Offer Expanded Opportunities for Developing and Assessing Musical Independence
- *Little Bells of Westminster* Makes Provision for 12 Students to Perform Independent Entrances (4 + 4 + 4) at 3 Levels of Difficulty (Lines 1, 2, 3).

Suggestion: Allow students to determine when to enter the round without help.

**1** **Little Bells of Westminster** (4-PART ROUND)

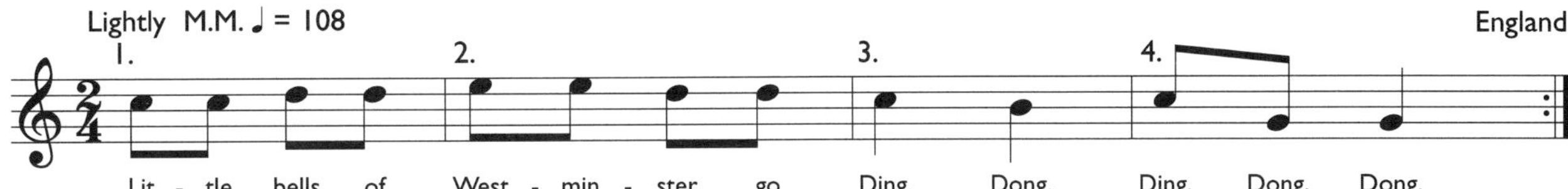


**2** **Variation One on *Little Bells of Westminster*** (4-PART ROUND)

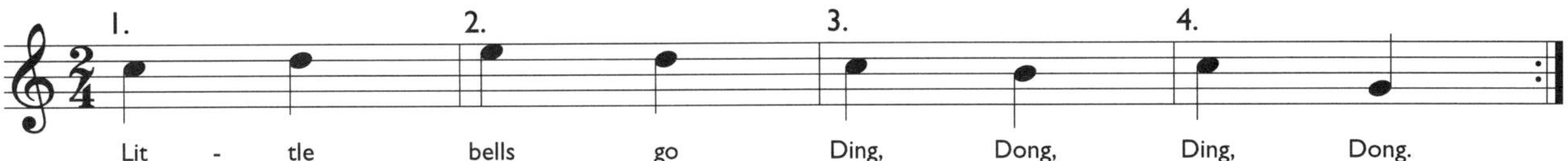


**3** **Variation Two on *Little Bells of Westminster*** (4-PART ROUND)

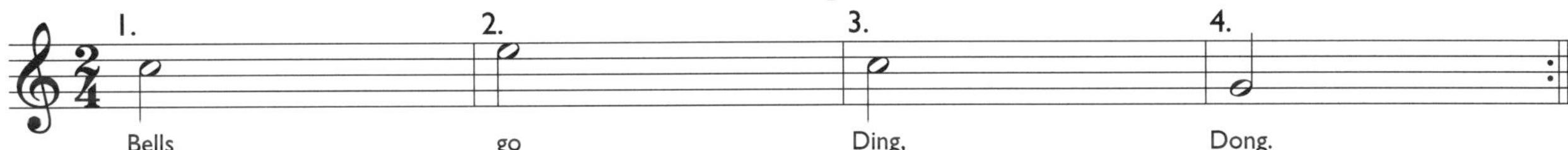


*Little Bells of Westminster, Variation One, and Variation Two may be played simultaneously.*

**4** **Two Birds** (4-PART ROUND)

**5** **Rooster Round** (5-PART ROUND)

# FOCUS ON TEACHING
## Success Is a Powerful Motivator

- Students need to have at least one acknowledged performance success during the course of every class.
- An easy variation can allow students to have a successful experience.
- An easy variation can give students motivation to practice for success with more challenging material.

Suggestion: Develop teaching strategies that orchestrate success in your classroom.

SPEAKER BALANCE
CONTROL
CD
Tr. 45
L R
Alto Saxophone
Accom.

**1 Hatikvah**

With expression

Hebrew Melody

Model Tr. 46
Accom. Tr. 46-1
High-Low

**2 Shoheen Sho**

Legato

Welsh Folk Song

**AURAL TRANSPOSITION** – *The process of playing a song or passage on a different starting note "by ear" without the aid of music notation.*

**3 SPECIAL PROJECT**

★SOLO★ *Hot Cross Buns "By Ear" Starting on F#*

English Folk Song

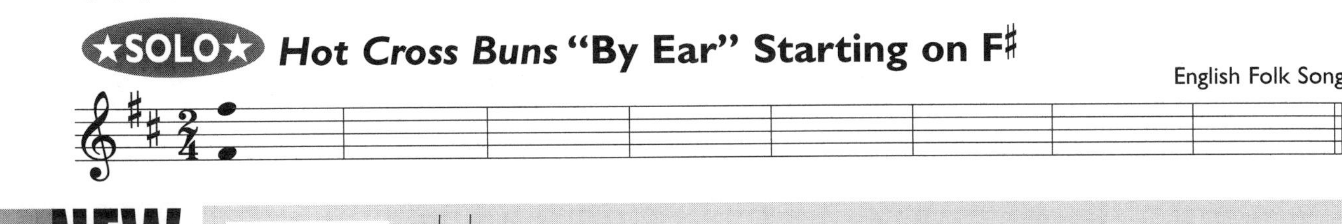


Play along
Tr. 47

**4 SPECIAL PROJECT – Let's Go Blue! – Play Along**

★SOLO★ **"By Ear" Use the tones G, B, C, C#, and D**

Accom. Tr. 33

**Tracking the Blues in F (Concert)**

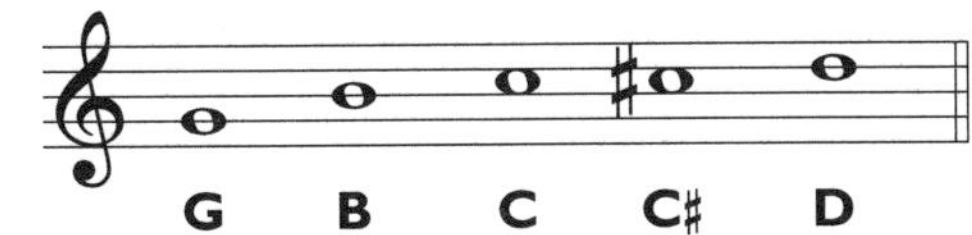

In a swinging style

**Model Tr. 48 / Accom. Tr. 48-1**

**❶ Bingo**

***BALLAD*** *– A short, simple song in a narrative or descriptive form, sometimes set to a romantic or historical poem.*

**Model Tr. 49 / Accom. Tr. 49-1**

**❷ Aura Lee**

***BLUES ROCK*** *– A musical style that merges blues harmonies with rock and roll rhythms of the 1950s and 1960s.*

**Call and Response Tr. 50**

**❸ SPECIAL PROJECT – Blues Rock "Call and Response"**

★SOLO★ **Blues Rock** (IMITATED RESPONSE) **Use the tones D, B, E, and F**

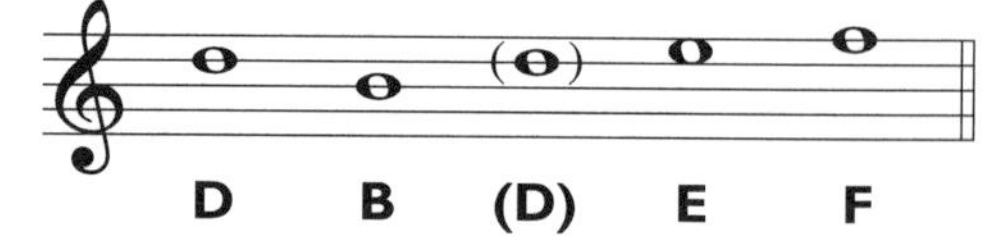


★SOLO★ **Blues Rock** (IMPROVISED RESPONSE) **Use the tones G, B, D, E, and F**

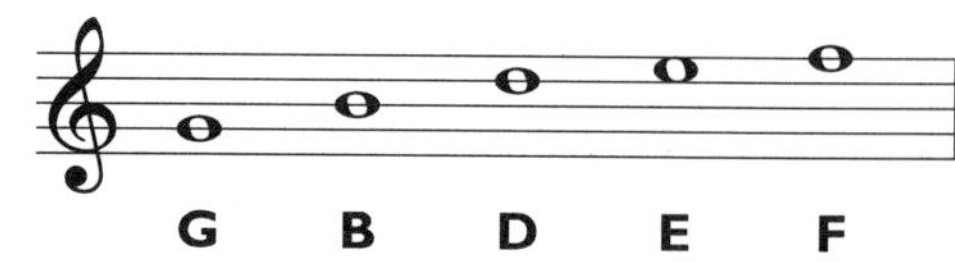

## 1 Old King Cole

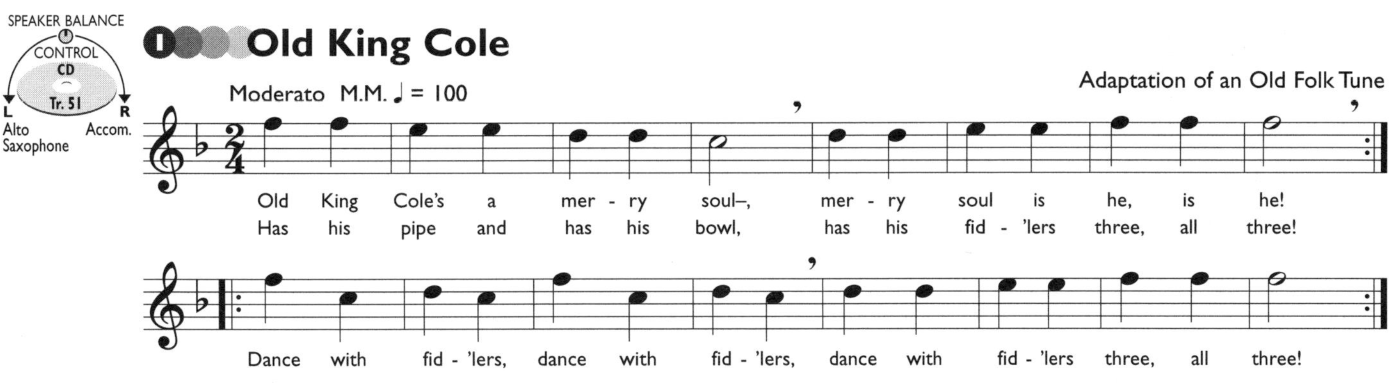


## 2 Bile 'em Cabbage Down

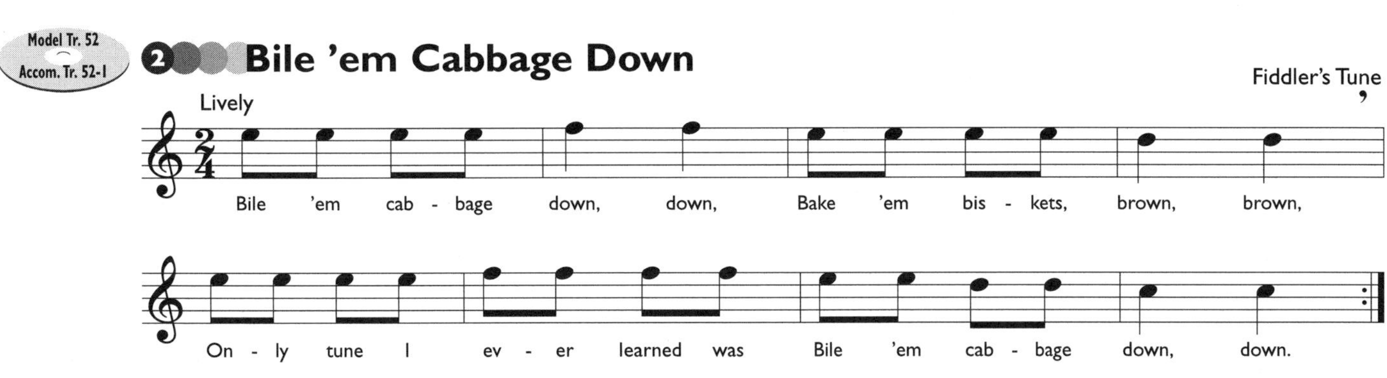


## 3 Now the Day Is Over

## 4 Yangtze Boatman Chanty

# NEW TONE:

SPEAKER BALANCE CONTROL CD Tr. 55 L R Alto Saxophone Accom.

## 1 Old King Cole

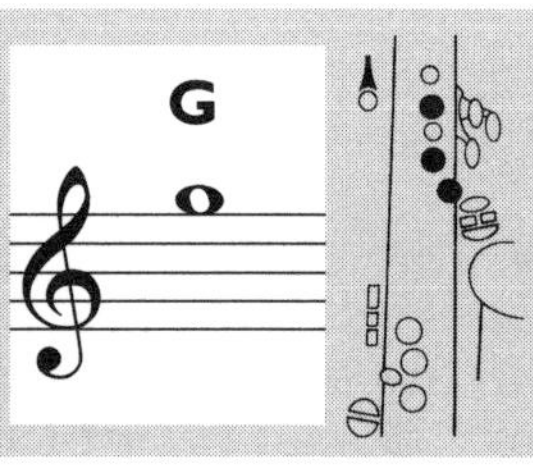

Moderato M.M. ♩ = 100

Adaptation of an Old Folk Tune

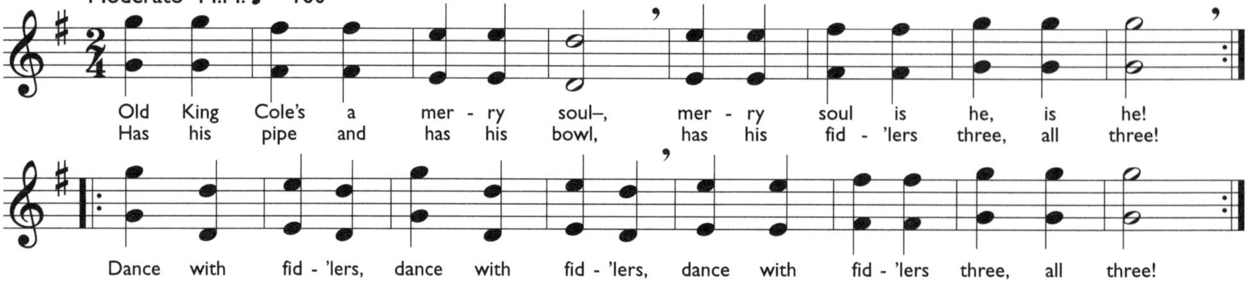


***BARCAROLLE** – Originally, a folk song of the Venetian gondoliers (boatmen of the Italian city of Venice).*

SPEAKER BALANCE CONTROL CD Tr. 56 L R Alto Saxophone Accom.

## 2 Barcarolle

Smoothly - In one

Jacques Offenbach (1819–1880)

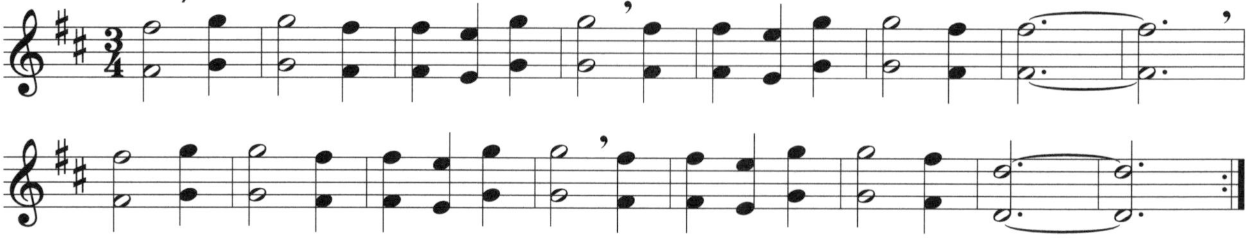

Model Tr. 57 Accom. Tr. 57-1

## 3 Jacob Drink

With enthusiasm

Polish Folk Song

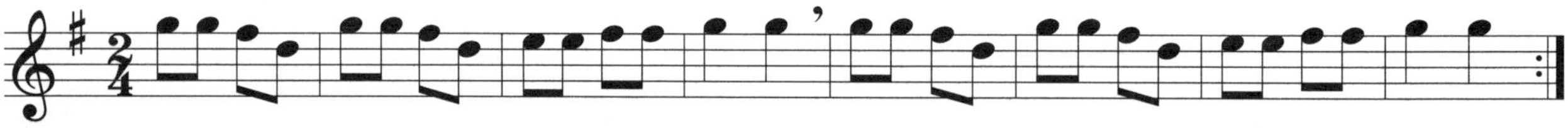

Accom. Tr. 57-1

## 4 Variation One on *Jacob Drink*

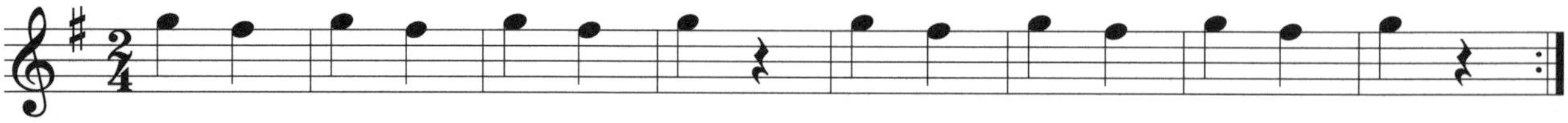

Accom. Tr. 57-1

## 5 Variation Two on *Jacob Drink*

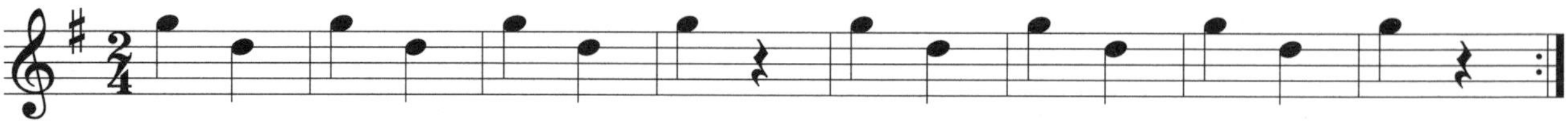

Accom. Tr. 57-1

## 6 Variation Three on *Jacob Drink*

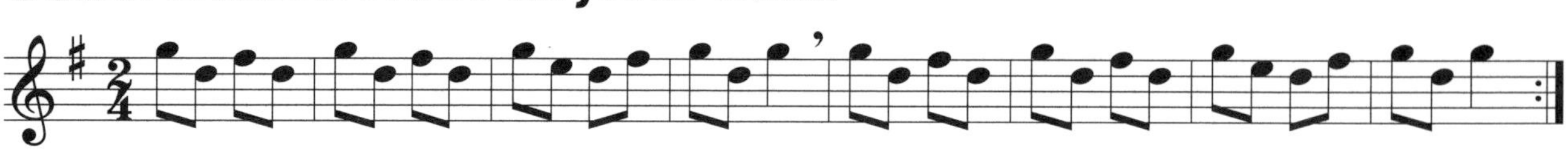

# NEW TONE:

Model Tr. 58 / Accom. Tr. 58-1

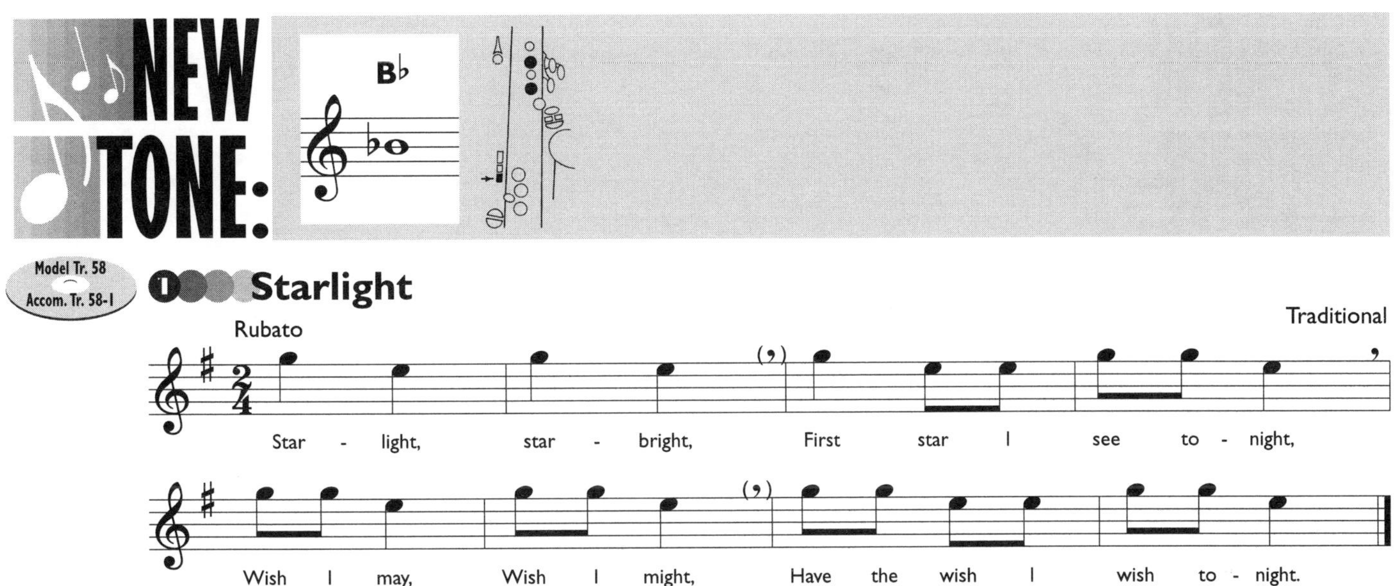

## 1 Starlight

Traditional

Rubato

***FOLK HYMN** – A song of worship with a religious text that has been set to a folk melody.*

SPEAKER BALANCE CONTROL CD Tr. 59 — L Alto Saxophone, R Accom.

## 2 Amazing Grace

John Newell (1779)
Early American Melody

Stately

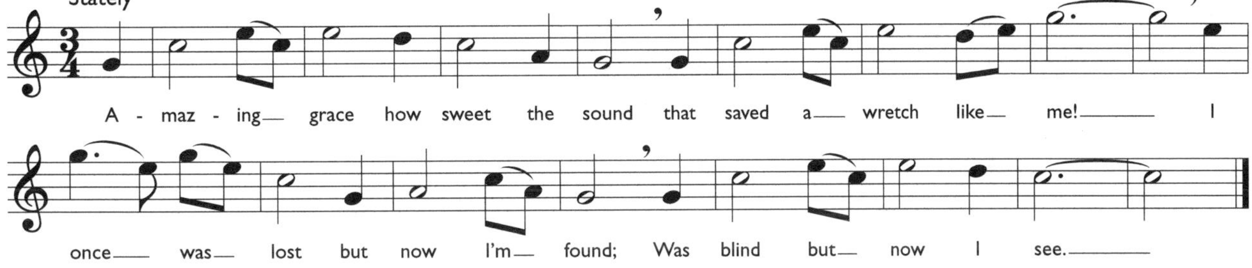

## 3 *Amazing Grace* Harmony Part One

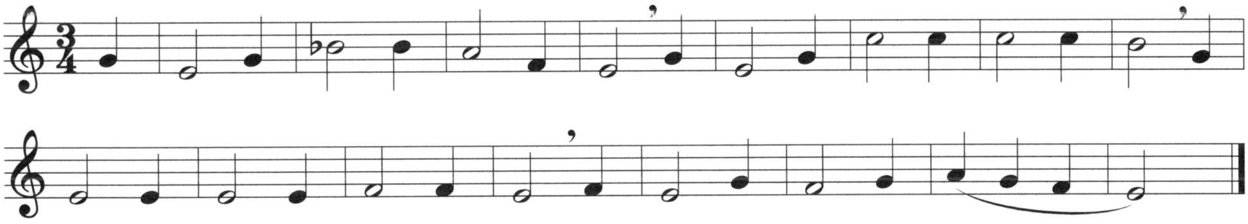

## 4 *Amazing Grace* Harmony Part Two

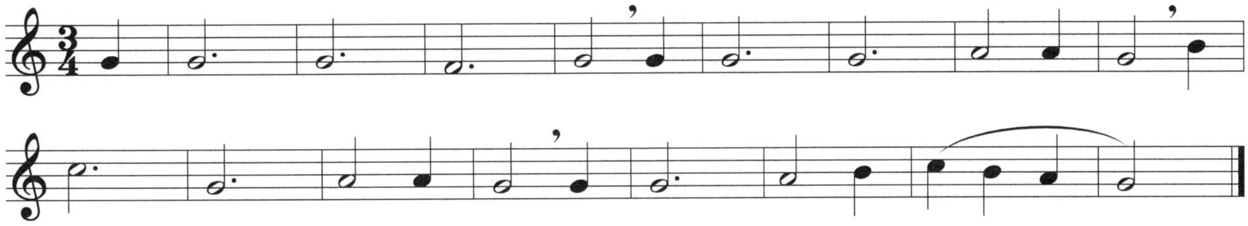

***GOSPEL** – African-American church music characterized by expression, improvisation, and a strong sense of celebration.*

Accom. Tr. 60

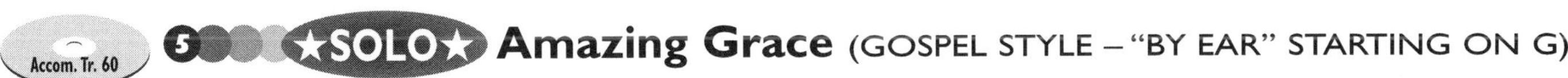

## 5 ★SOLO★ Amazing Grace (GOSPEL STYLE – "BY EAR" STARTING ON G)

Accom. Tr. 60

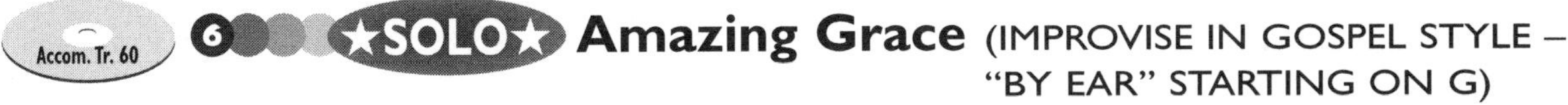

## 6 ★SOLO★ Amazing Grace (IMPROVISE IN GOSPEL STYLE – "BY EAR" STARTING ON G)

**Model Tr. 61 / Accom. Tr. 62**

## 1 Scarborough Fair (DORIAN MODE)

English Ballad

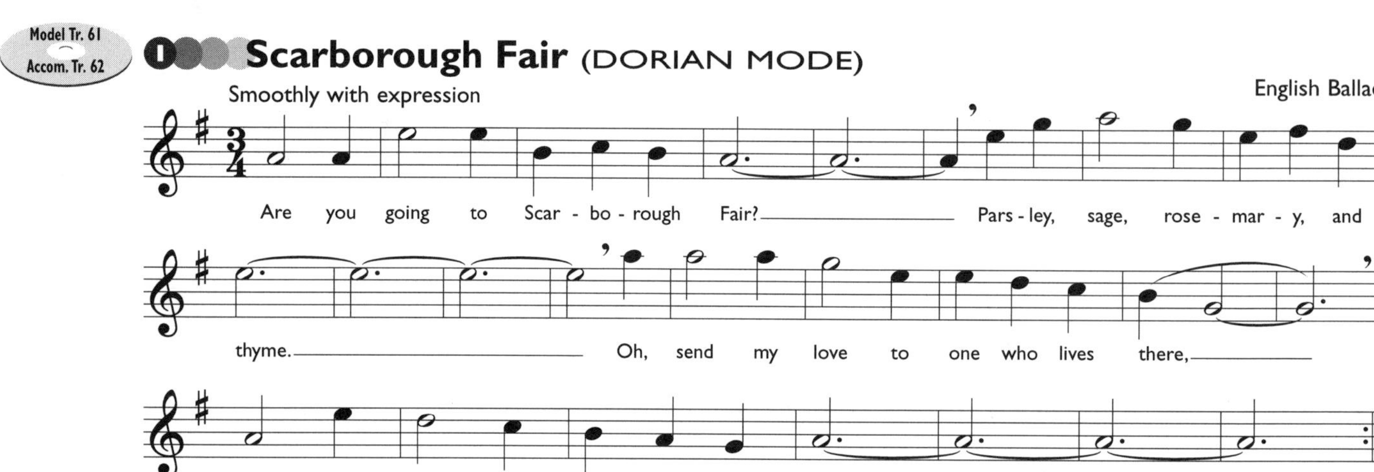


## 2 The Hart, He Loves the High Wood (4-PART ROUND)

Composer Unknown ca. 1680

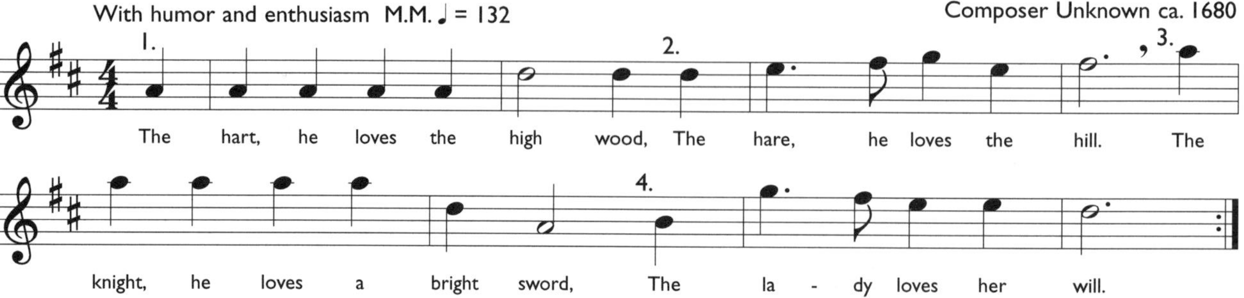


## 3 Row, Row, Row Your Boat (4-PART ROUND)

U.S.
E. O. Lyte

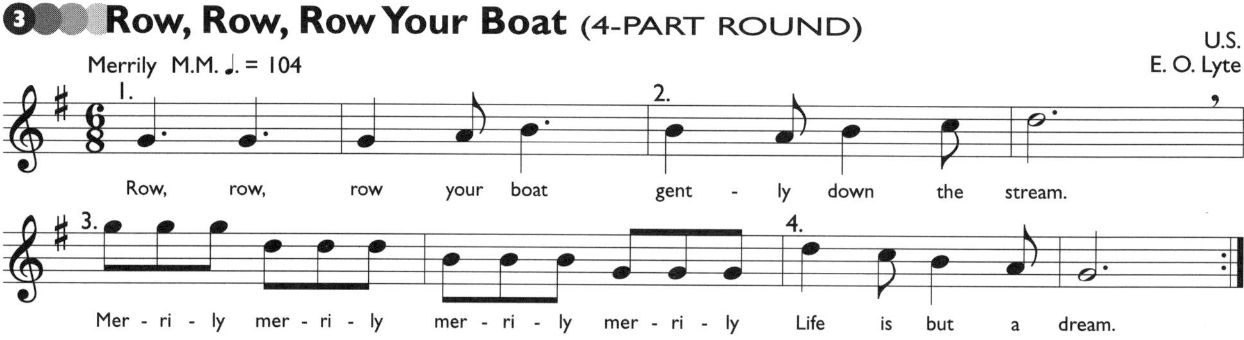


## 4 Time and Tide (2-PART ROUND)

Lowell Mason (1864)

## 5 Shave and a Haircut

Early American

# FOCUS ON TEACHING

## Musical Models and Accompaniments Provide Opportunities to Teach:

**Tone Quality**

**Intonation**

**Phrasing**

**Articulation**

**Expressive Nuance**

**Dynamics**

**Rhythm**

**Melody**

**Harmony**

**Form**

**Style**

**Music Culture**

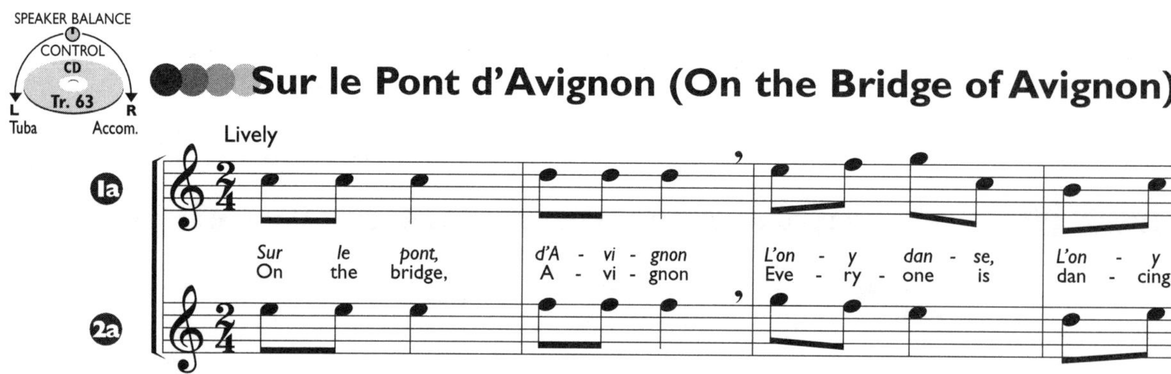

SPEAKER BALANCE
CONTROL
CD
Tr. 63
L    R
Tuba    Accom.
Sur le Pont d'Avignon (On the Bridge of Avignon) Duet
French Folk Song
Lively
1a
2a
Sur    le    pont,    d'A - vi - gnon    L'on - y    dan - se,    L'on - y    dan - se.
On    the    bridge,    A - vi - gnon    Eve - ry - one is    dan - cing,    dan - cing.
1b
2b
Sur - le - pont,    d'A - vi - gnon    L'on - y    dan - se,    tout en rond.
On    the    bridge,    A - vi - gnon    They    are    dan - cing    in a    round.

3 Melodic Ostinatos to Sur le Pont d'Avignon
a    4 times
b    4 times
c    4 times
d    4 times

4 Singing Goose (4-PART ROUND)
Moderato M.M. ♩ = 100
England
1.
Why    should - n't    my    goose,    Sing    as    well    as    thy    goose,
2.
3.
When    I    paid    for    my    goose,    Twice    as    much    as    thou?
4.

5 Santy Maloney (4-PART ROUND)
Spirited M.M. ♩ = 100
England
1.
Can    you    dance    San - ty    Ma - lon - ey?    Can    you    dance    San - ty    Ma - lon - ey?
2.
3.
Can    you    dance    San - ty    Ma - lon - ey,    As    we    go    round    a - bout?
4.

*HIGH LIFE* – *A popular song and dance style of West Africa (Ghana) that blends African and Western instruments and musical characteristics; it can occur in duple or triple meter and features rhythmic and melodic ostinati.*

**Play Along Tr. 64**

**1.** **Banuwa** (3-PART ROUND)

West Africa (Liberia)

Joyously

**Play Along Tr. 65**

**2.** **Lotus Blossoms**

Rhythmically

**SPEAKER BALANCE CONTROL CD Tr. 66** — L Clarinet / R Accom.

**Hat Dance from Mexico** (DUET)

Mexican Folk Dance

Spirited

**3a** **4a** **3b** **4b**

**SPECIAL PROJECT**

**★SOLO★ Learn to Play Line 3 of *Hat Dance from Mexico* 8va Lower**

**5.** **Shalom Chaverim** (8-PART ROUND)

Israel

Stately M.M. ♩ = 92

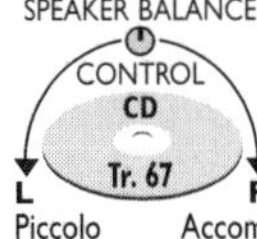

**6.** **SPECIAL PROJECT – Learn to Play a Song "By Ear"**

**★SOLO★ Play *Yankee Doodle* Starting on C** and **D**

SPEAKER BALANCE CONTROL CD Tr. 67 — L Piccolo / R Accom.

## 50

*SAMBA* – *A Brazilian dance music form in duple meter.*

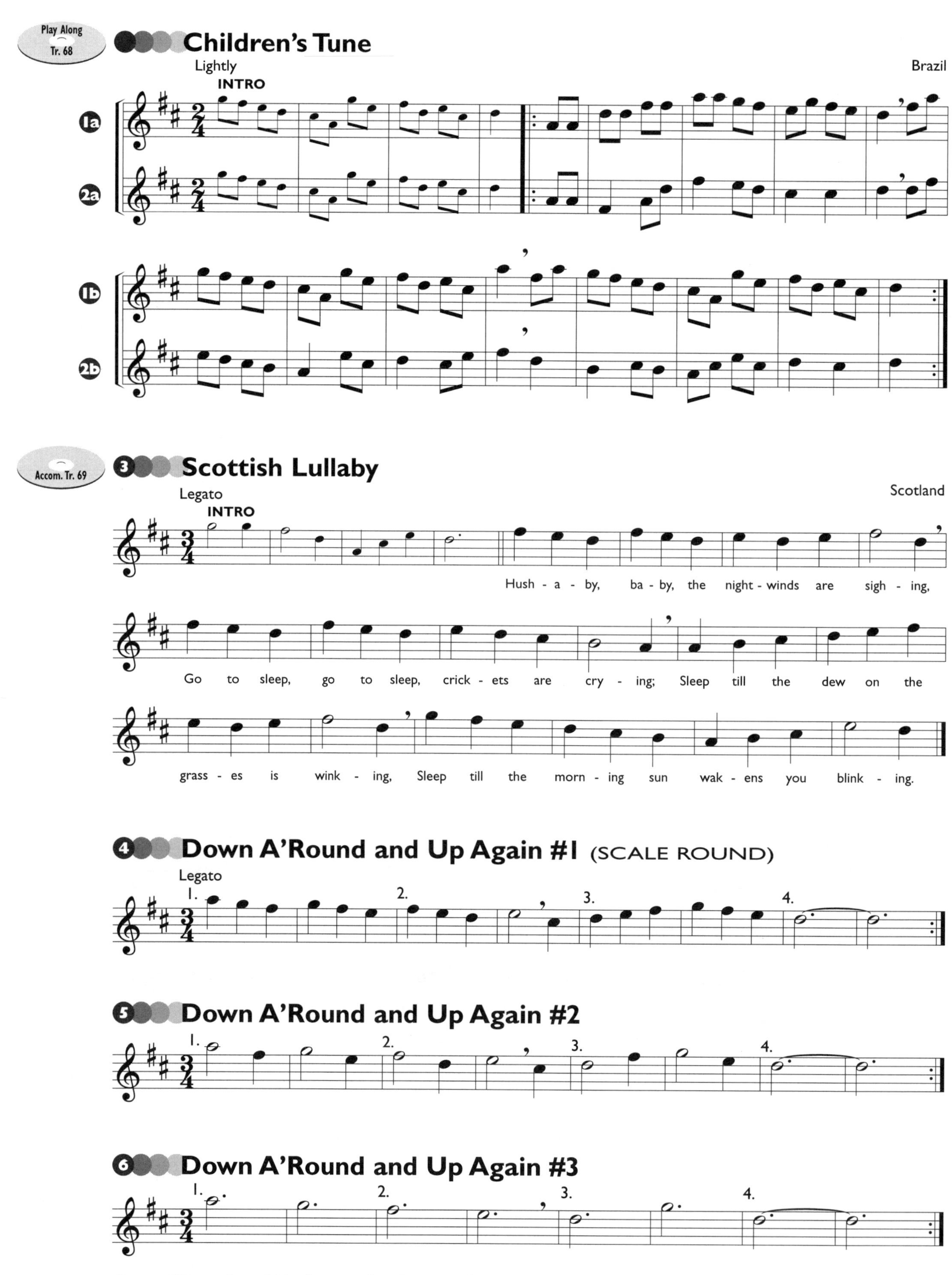



*Down A'Round and Up Again #1, #2, and #3 may be played simultaneously.*

*PARTNER SONGS** – *Songs that may be played simultaneously to a common accompaniment.*

****A-Workin' on the Railroad; Oats, Peas, Beans; Bluebird; and The Mulberry Bush are Partner Songs***

### ❶ A-Workin' on the Railroad

### ❷ Oats, Peas, Beans

### ❸ Bluebird

### ❹ The Mulberry Bush

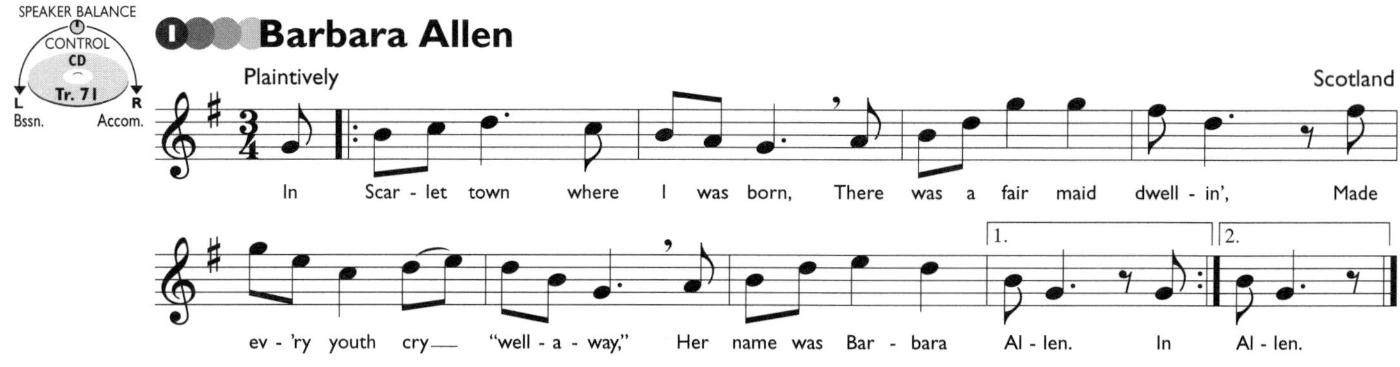

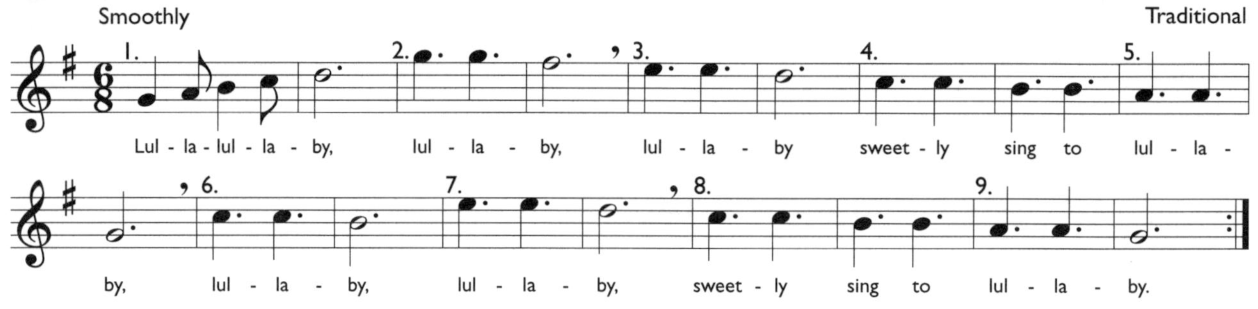

5 SPECIAL PROJECT – Return to *Cobbler, Cobbler* on Page 31 to Improvise

# FOCUS ON TEACHING

## A Special Individualized Option for Spontaneous Music Making

### Cobbler, Cobbler

*MUSICAL PARAPHRASE* – *An improvised conversation between two performers. The conversation begins with a 4-beat improvised "Call." The "Response" is a 4-beat restatement (paraphrase) of the "Call" using a slightly different combination of tones, rhythm, and/or articulations.*

**Direct students to employ one of the following options:**

### EXAMPLE OF OPTION A:

"The starting note is D"

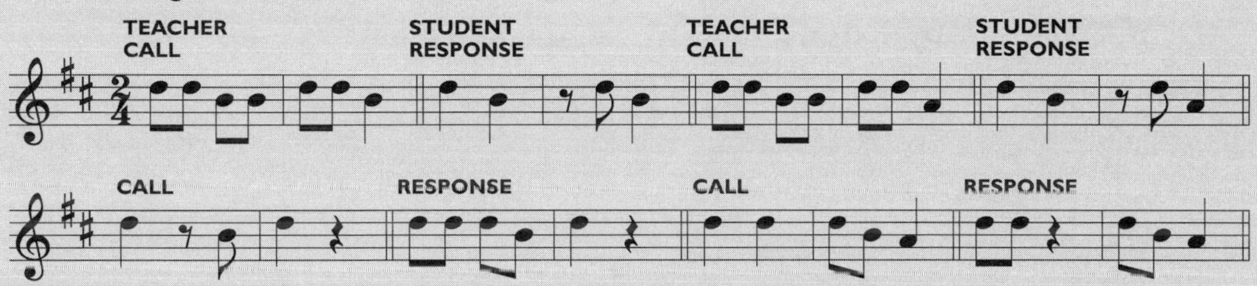


**Suggestion:** To reduce student apprehension, involve students in group paraphrased responses.

### EXAMPLE OF OPTION B:

"The starting note is D"

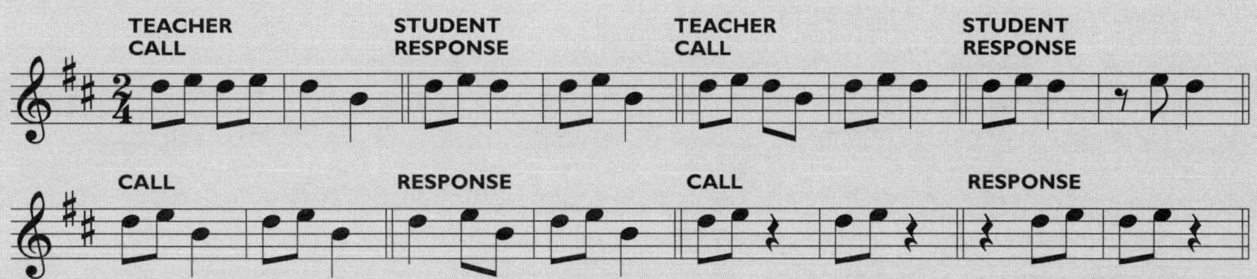


**Suggestion:** Always ask for volunteers when engaging in individual student paraphrased responses.

## Another Option for Spontaneous Music Making

- Ask volunteers to lead the class with their own improvised calls (vocal or instrumental).

- Direct the class to follow with imitated or improvised responses.

### 1. Greensleeves

### 2. Lullaby Round (9-PART SCALE ROUND)

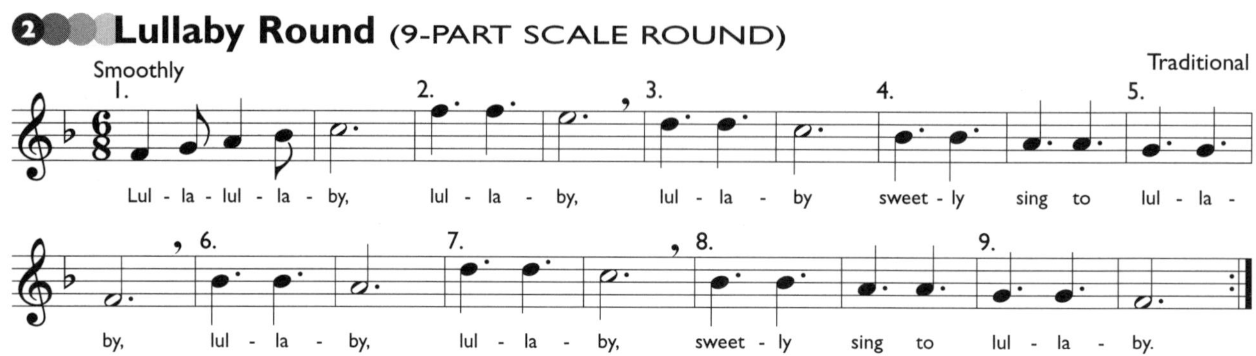


### 3. Rise Up, O Flame (4-PART ROUND)

### 4. Blow the Winds Southerly (4-PART SCALE ROUND)

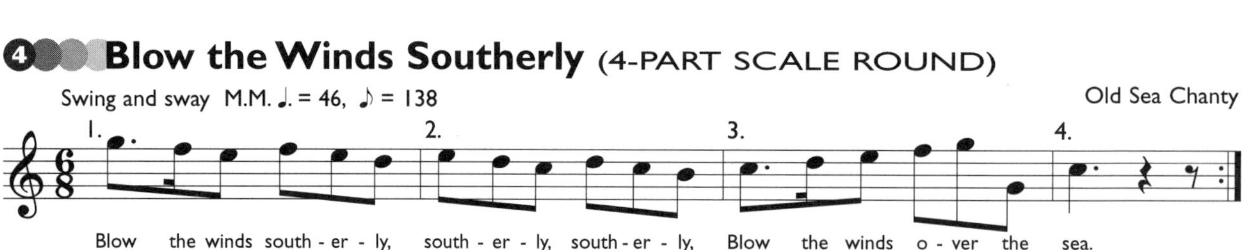

## Saint Paul's Steeple (SCALE SONG AND DUET)

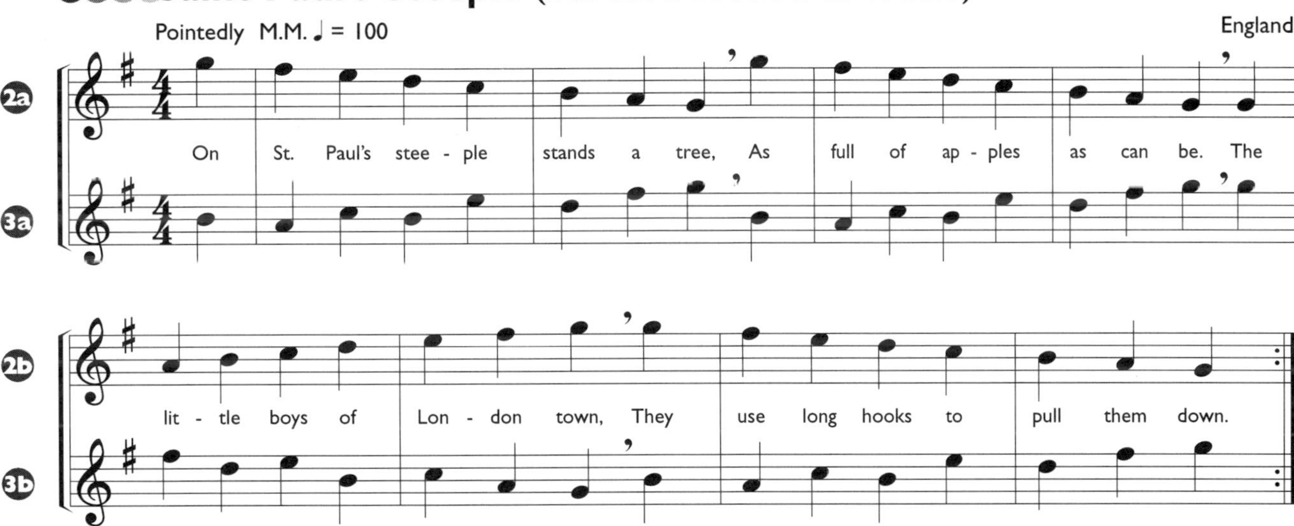


## Chumbara (SCALE SONG)

# NEW TONE:

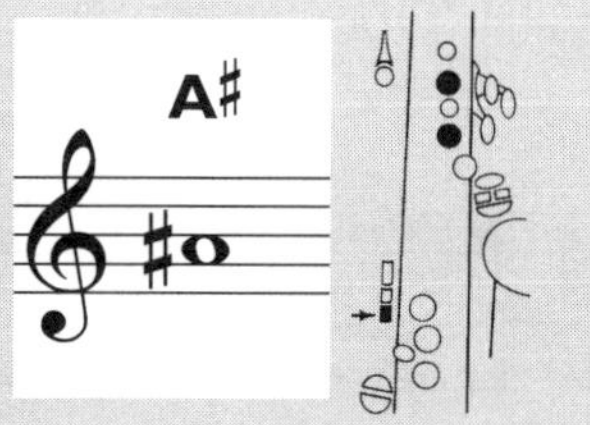

*SEIS – A traditional song of dance music style of Puerto Rico in duple meter.*

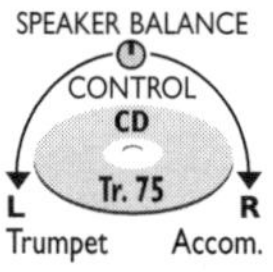


## 1 Habemos Llegado (PLAY ALONG)

Lightly

Puerto Rican Folk Song

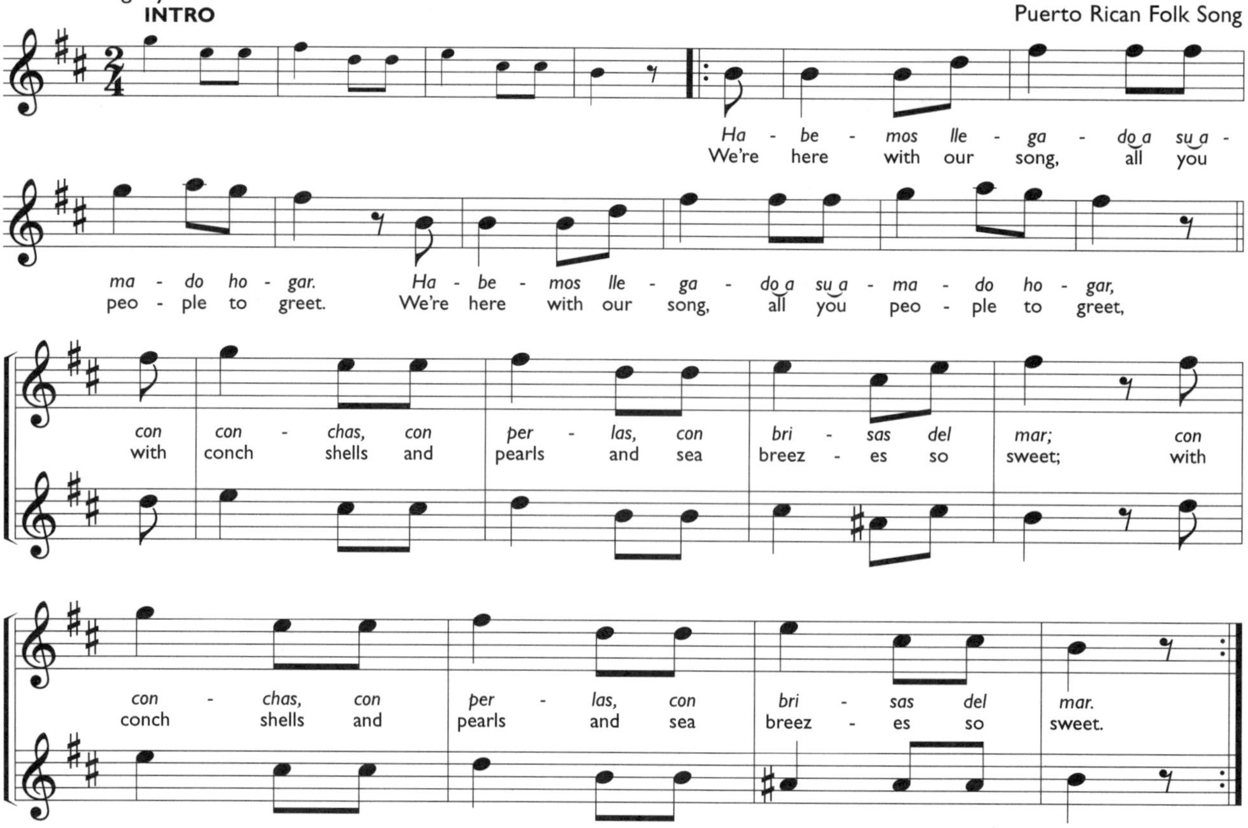


## 3 Aeolian Scale (NATURAL MINOR SCALE)

M.M. ♩ = 88

## 4 Old Abram Brown (NATURAL MINOR SCALE ROUND)

Heavy and sad M.M. ♩ = 88

Traditional

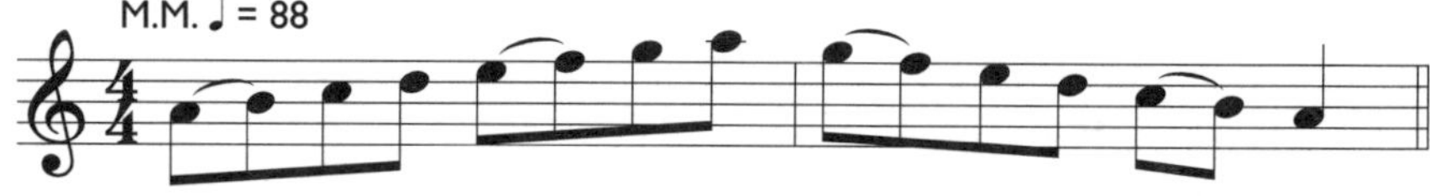

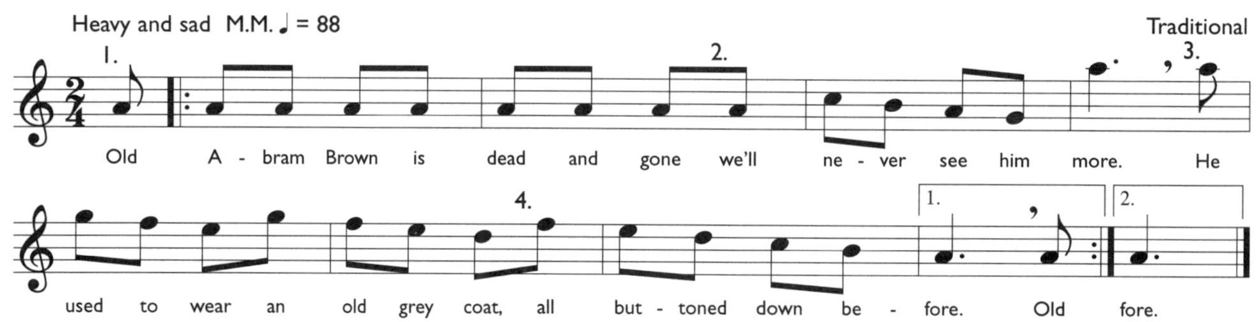

***SYNCOPATION*** – *A displacement of the natural pulse or accent of the music, usually to the second half of the beat, as in:* ♪ ♩. *and* ♪ ♩ ♪

## SPECIAL PROJECT – "Call and Response"

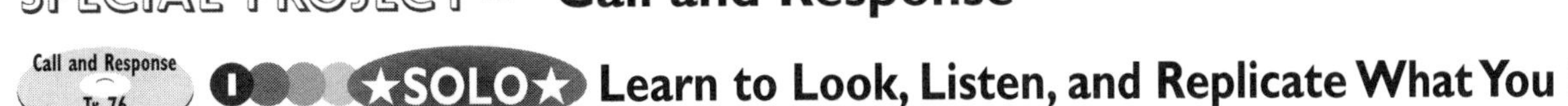


### Do As I Do

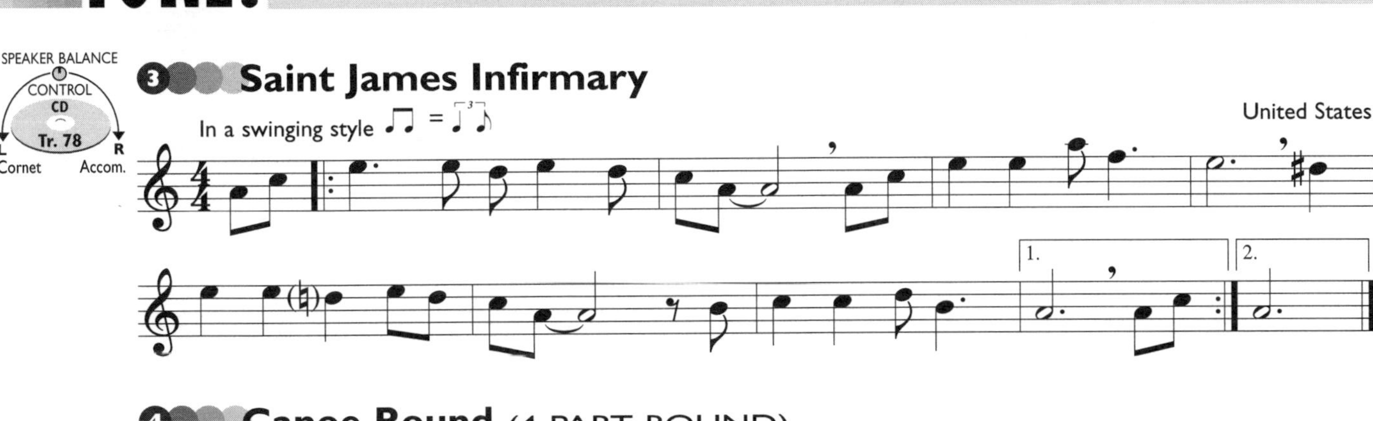


### ❹ Canoe Round (4-PART ROUND)

58

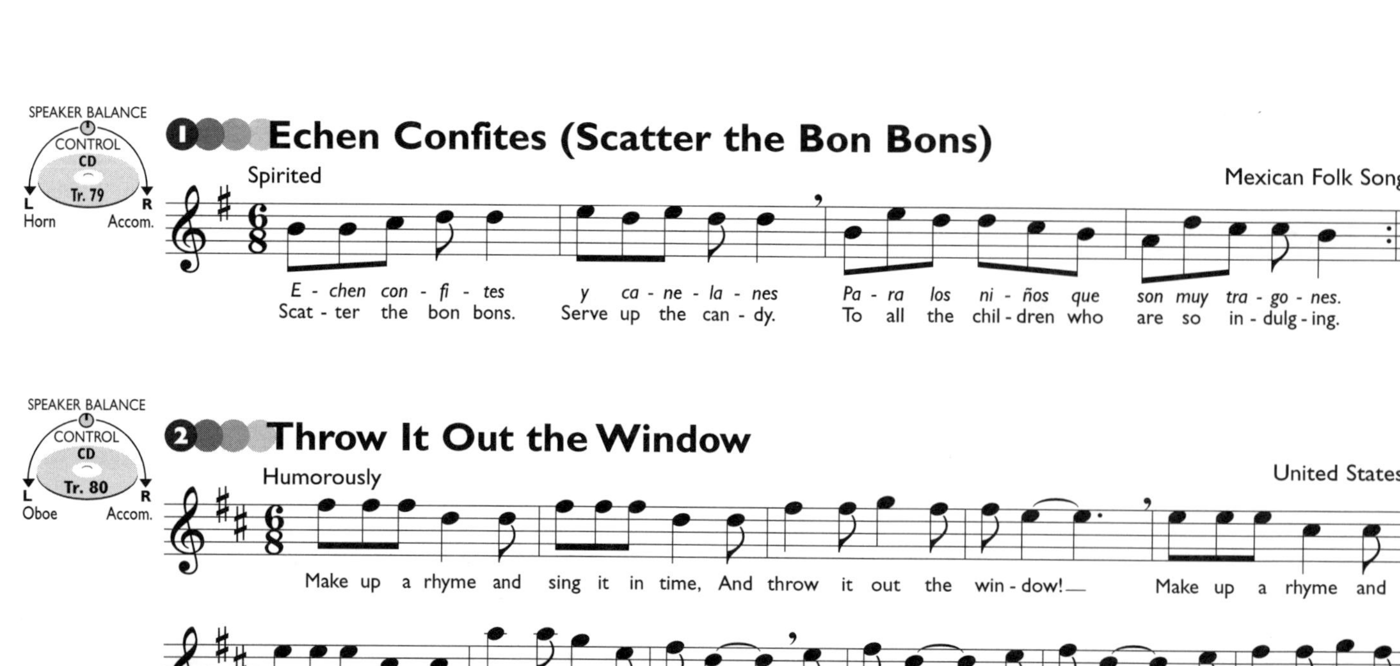
SPEAKER BALANCE
CONTROL
CD
Tr. 79
L Horn   R Accom.

1 Echen Confites (Scatter the Bon Bons)
Spirited
Mexican Folk Song

E - chen con - fi - tes    y   ca - ne - la - nes    Pa - ra  los  ni - ños  que   son muy tra - go - nes.
Scat - ter  the bon bons.   Serve  up  the can - dy.   To  all  the chil - dren who   are  so  in - dulg - ing.

SPEAKER BALANCE
CONTROL
CD
Tr. 80
L Oboe   R Accom.

2 Throw It Out the Window
Humorously
United States

Make up a rhyme and  sing it in time, And throw  it  out  the win - dow! ___   Make  up  a  rhyme and

sing it in time, And throw  it out the win - dow!  The  win - dow, ___  the  win - dow, ___  the  sec - ond sto - ry

win - dow. ___   Make  up  a  rhyme  and  sing it in time  and  throw  it  out  the  win - dow! ___

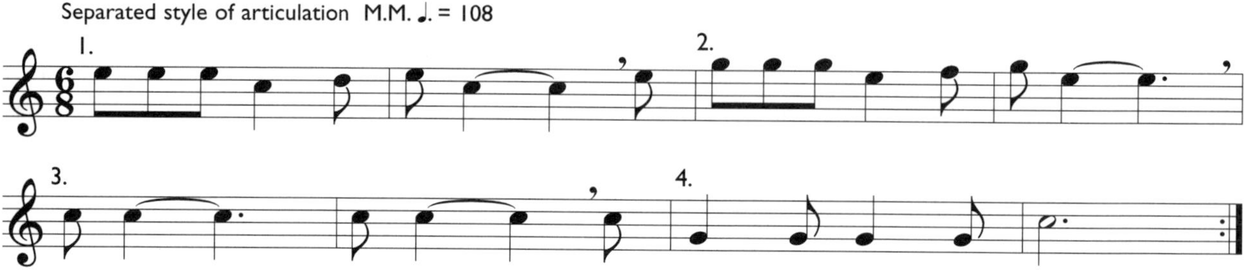
3 Throw It! A Round
Separated style of articulation  M.M. ♩. = 108

1.                                        2.

3.                                        4.

SPEAKER BALANCE
CONTROL
CD
Tr. 81
L Horn   R Accom.

4 Rig-A-Jig-Jig
Lightly
INTRO
United States

As    I  was walk - ing  down  the  street,   Down  the  street,

down  the  street, A  pret - ty girl I  chanced  to  meet,  Hi - ho, hi - ho, hi - ho.

(♩ = ♩.)

Rig - a - jig - jig  and  a - way  we  go,  A - way  we  go,  A - way  we  go.

Rig - a - jig - jig  and  a - way  we  go.  Hi - ho,  hi - ho, ___  hi - ho.

## African Farewell (CALL AND RESPONSE)

## Canon (C MAJOR SCALE CANON IN 6 PARTS)

## Hallelujah (C MAJOR SCALE ROUND IN 2 PARTS)

## SPECIAL PROJECT – Learn To Play *Lullaby Round* Starting on A

## ❶ Scale Duet (A HARMONIC MINOR SCALE DUET)

**KLEZMER** – *A term that refers to a popular style of Jewish instrumetnal music.*

## ❷ Rozhinkes mit Mandlen (Raisins and Almonds)

## ❸ A La Nanita Nana

## ❹ Ah, Poor Bird (4-PART ROUND)

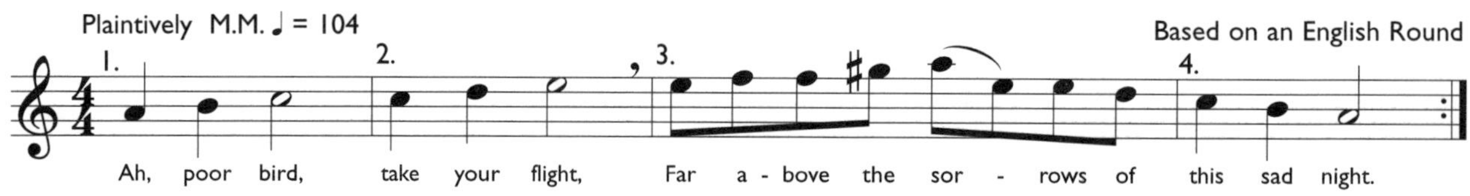



## ❺ SPECIAL PROJECT – Return to *Cobbler, Cobbler* on Page 31 to Improvise

# FOCUS ON TEACHING

## A Special Individualized Option for Spontaneous Music Making

 **Cobbler, Cobbler**

*MUSICAL DIALOGUE* – *A type of improvised Call and Response between two performers.*

The musical dialogue, like the musical paraphrase, is an improvised conversation between two performers. A performer initiates a *Dialogue* with a 4-beat improvised *Statement* or a 4-beat improvised *Question*. A second performer responds with a 4-beat improvised *Answer*, a 4-beat improvised *Statement*, or a 4-beat improvised *Question*.

A musical **Statement** usually starts on the resting tone and always ends on the resting tone (D is the resting tone for *Cobbler, Cobbler*).

A musical **Answer** usually starts on a tone other than the resting tone and always ends on the resting tone.

A musical **Question** can begin on any tone but always ends on a tone other than the resting tone.

**Direct students to employ one of the following options:**

**A.** "Use the tones D, B, and A" or

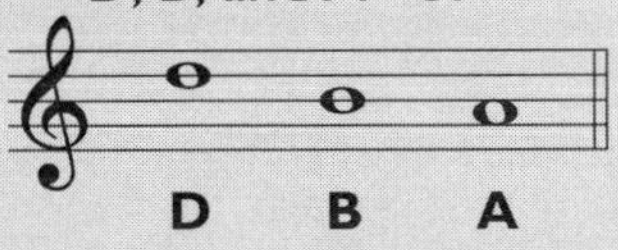

**B.** "Use the tones D, E, B, and A" or

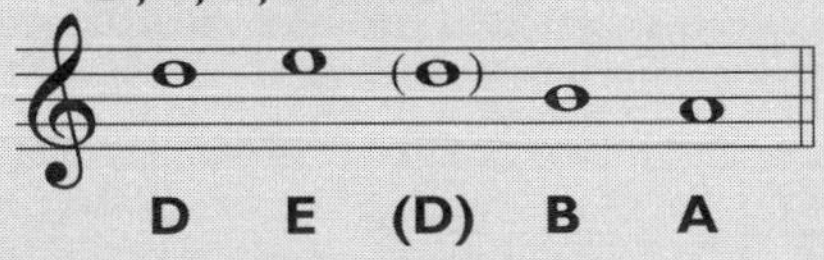

**C.** "Use the tones D, E, B, A, and F♯"

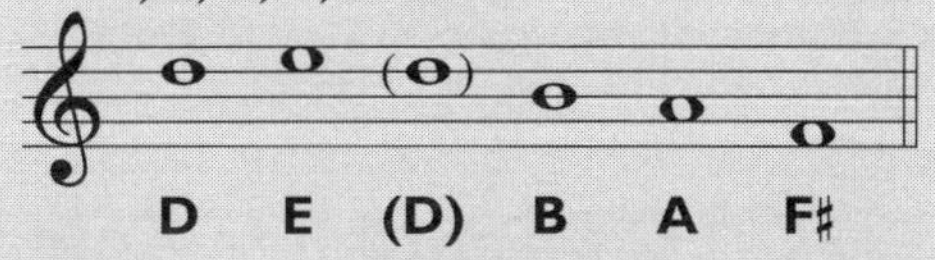

### EXAMPLE OF OPTION A:

### EXAMPLE OF OPTION B:

### EXAMPLE OF OPTION C:

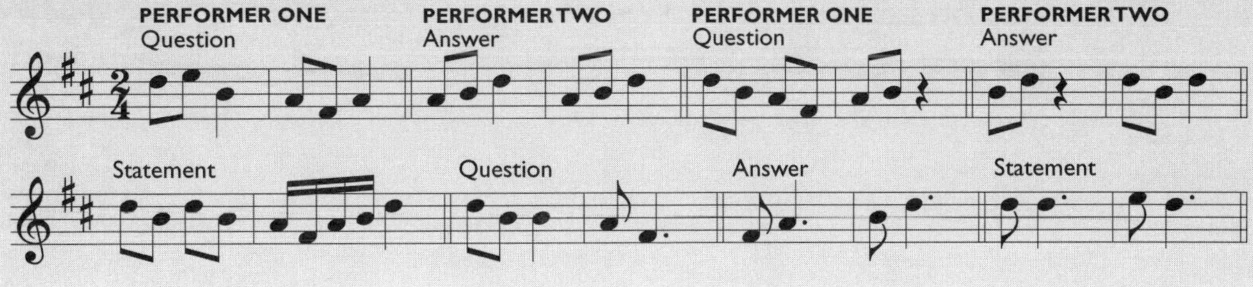

## ❶ Ticky Tacky Houses (PLAY ALONG)

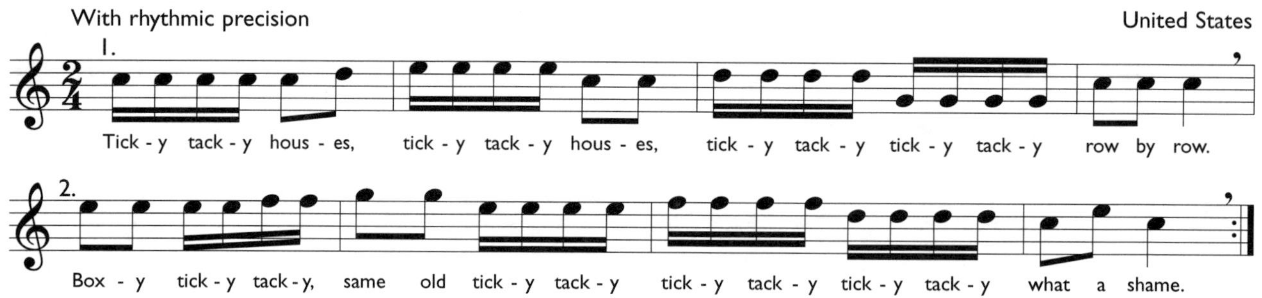


## ❷ Clocks (3-PART ROUND)

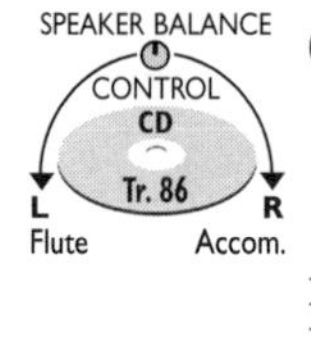


## ❸ Soldier, Soldier

## ❹ Christmas Is Coming (3-PART ROUND)

**PARTNER SONGS*** – *Songs that may be played simultaneously to a common accompaniment.*

***When the Saints Go Marching In; This Train; and Swing Low,
Sweet Chariot are Partner Songs**

### ❶ When the Saints Go Marching In

### ❷ This Train

### ❸ Swing Low, Sweet Chariot

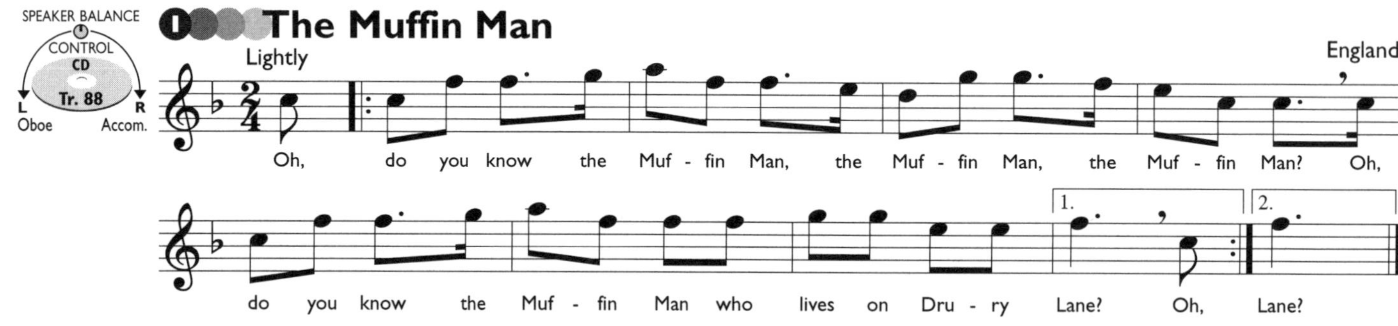


# FOCUS ON TEACHING
## Interpreting Music Signs and Symbols

**Music signs and symbols should not be interpreted literally, for example:**

- $\frac{3}{4}$ may be conducted in one or three; it is open to interpretation
- $\frac{6}{8}$ may be conducted in two or six; it is open to interpretation
- $\frac{4}{4}$ may be conducted in four or two; it is open to interpretation
- $\frac{2}{4}$ ♫ ♫ may be performed with an even subdivision or in a swinging style; it is open to interpretation
- $\frac{2}{4}$ may be performed with an even subdivision or in the style of a swinging "shuffle;" it is open to interpretation

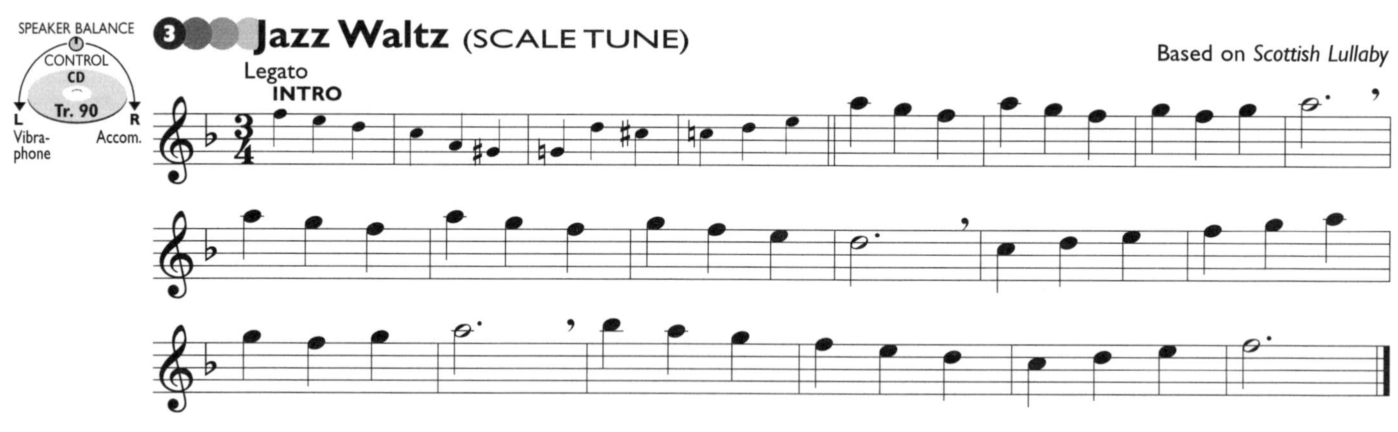

**PARTNER SONGS*** – *Songs that may be played simultaneously to a common accompaniment.*

***This Old Man, Pawpaw Patch, Old Brass Wagon, and Bow Belinda are Partner Songs**

**1 College Mascots**

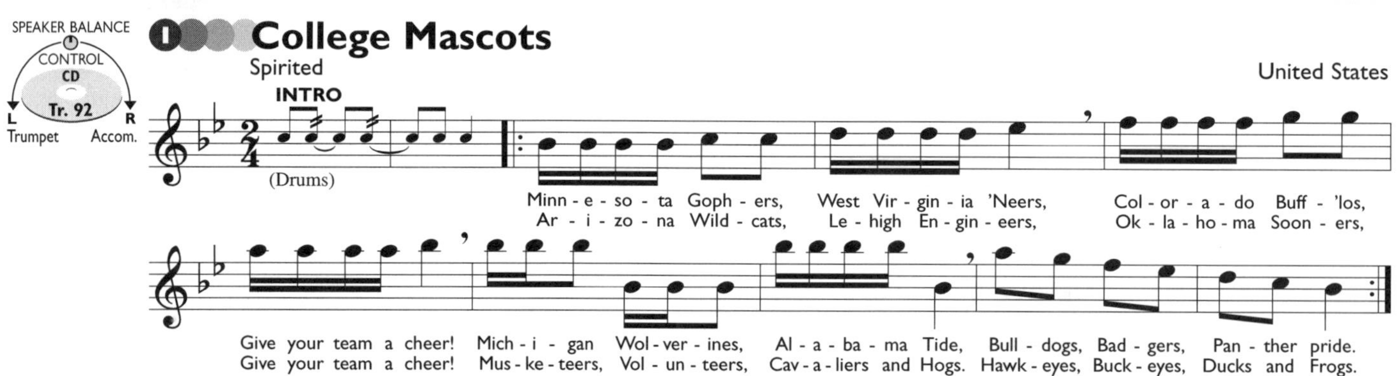


**ALTERNATIVE FINGERING:**

**2 Shenandoah**

*CALYPSO* — A song style of Trinidad characterized by dry, witty texts and traditional steel band accompaniment.

**3 Mary Ann (PLAY ALONG)**

# FOCUS ON TEACHING
## Connecting What Is Known to What Is Unknown

Each pair looks different, yet sounds the same.

1a → 1b
2a → 2b
3a → 3b

# NEW TONE:

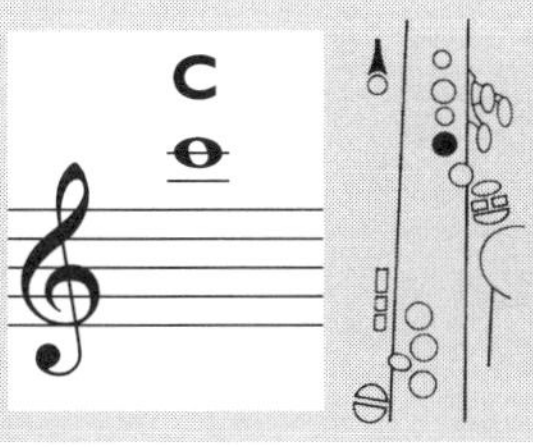

***POLKA*** *– A lively round dance originated by Bohemian (Eastern European) peasants.*

Accom. Tr. 95

## 1 Do It! (If You Can) Polka

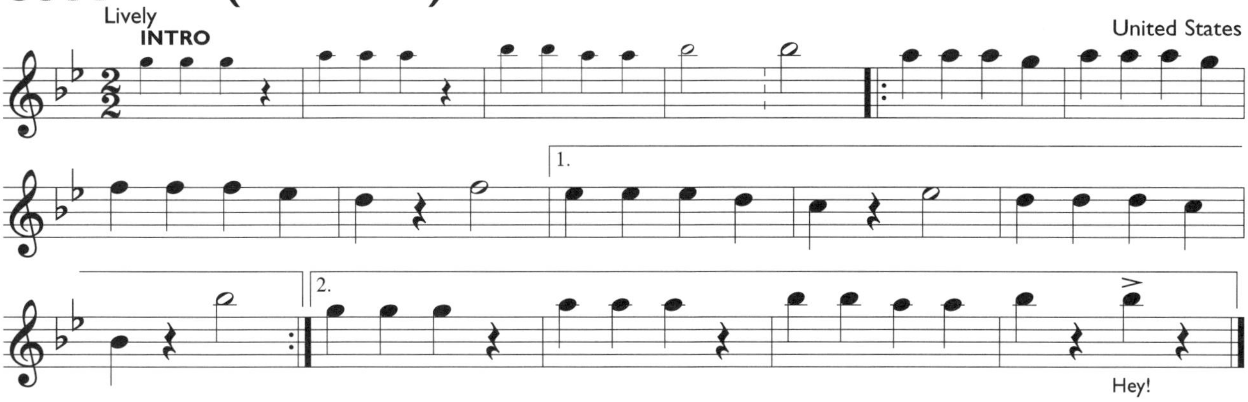


Accom. Tr. 95

## 2 Do It! Again (If You Can) Polka (SCALE VARIATION)

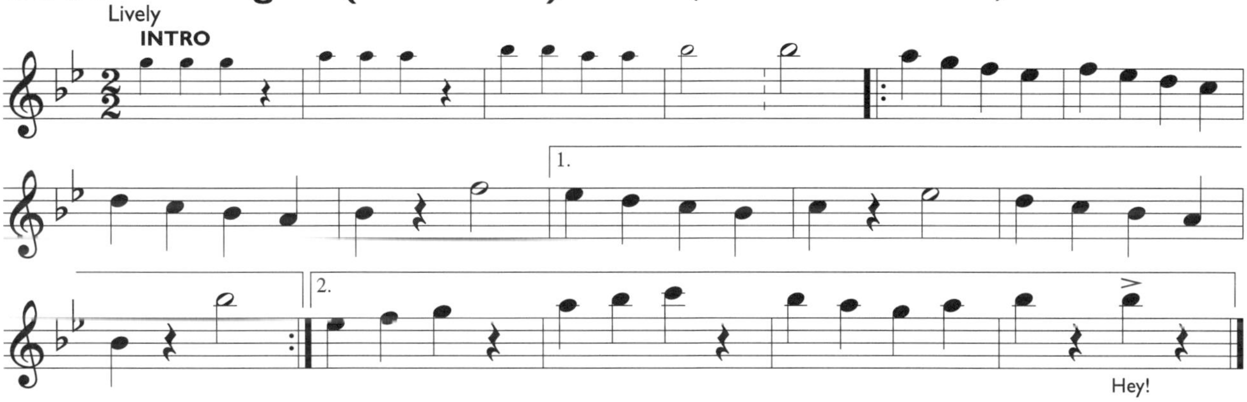


Accom. Tr. 95

## 3 Do It! Once More (If You Can) Polka

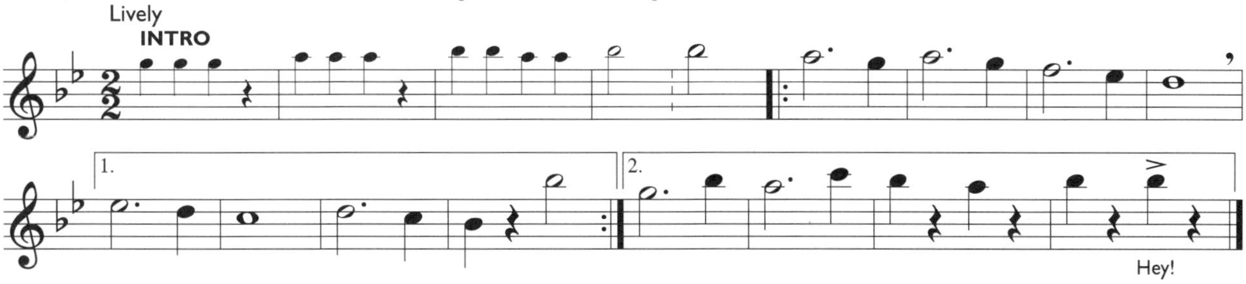


## 4 Kookaburra (4-PART ROUND)

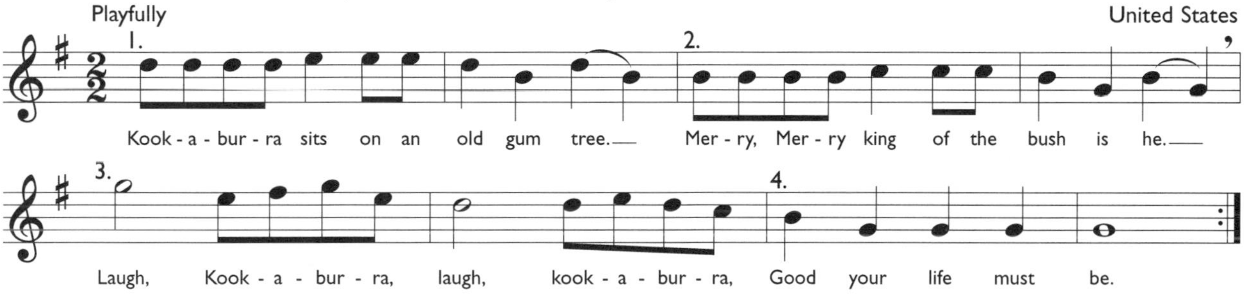


Each pair looks different, yet sounds the same.

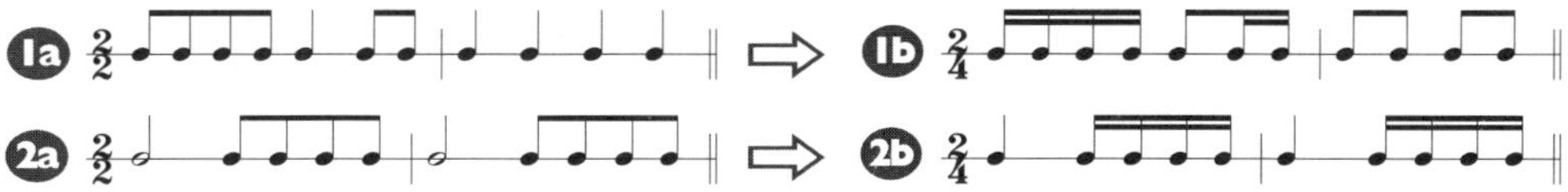

***ENHARMONIC NOTES*** *– Notes that sound the same though named or spelled differently.*

Each pair looks different, yet sounds the same

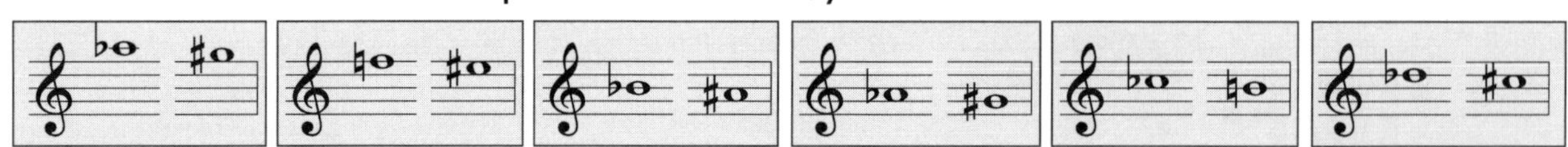



### ❶ Glow Worm

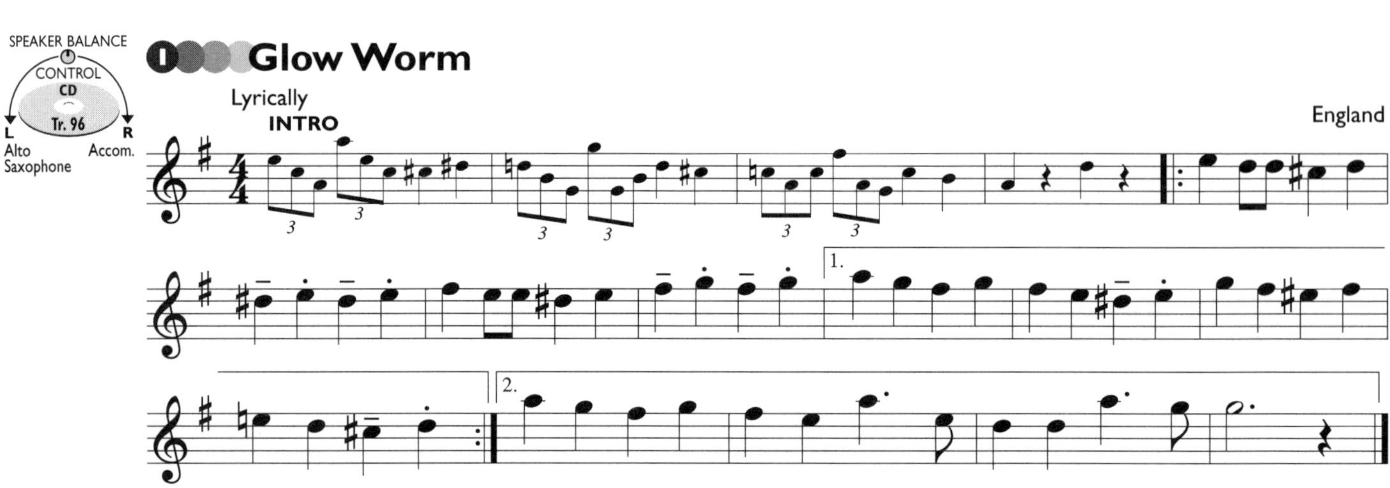


***GEORGES BIZET (1838–1875)*** *– French composer; he is perhaps best known for his opera Carmen.*

***TRIPLET*** *– Three notes of equal rhythmic value grouped together with a "3" over or under them.*

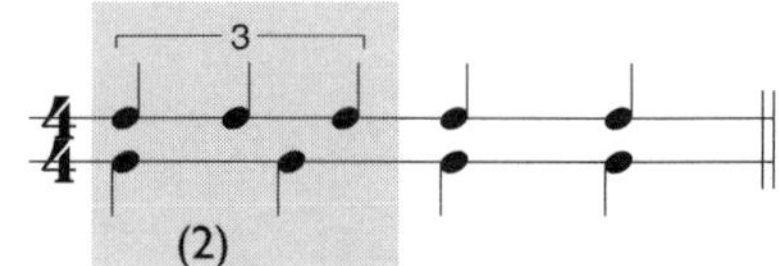

***HEMIOLA*** *– Literally, three against two. In 4 time signature, a hemiola is represented by three quarter notes performed evenly during the same duration as 2 quarter notes.*

### ❷ Habanera (FROM THE OPERA CARMEN)

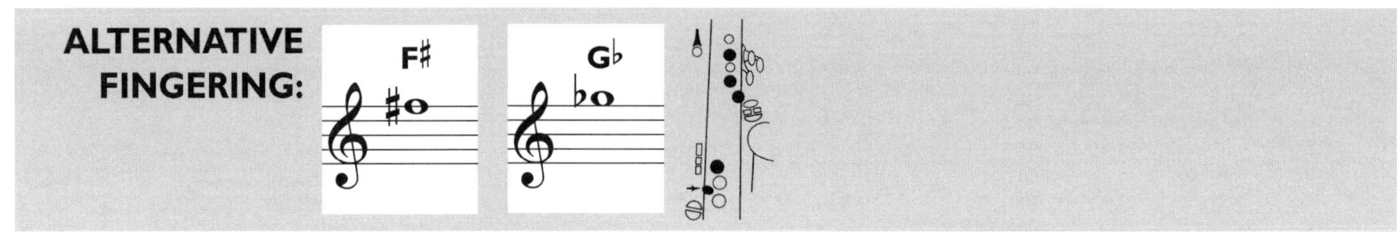



### ❷ Chromatic Scale

**1 Saint Anthony Chorale** (MELODY – FOR SOLO OR ENSEMBLE PERFORMANCE)

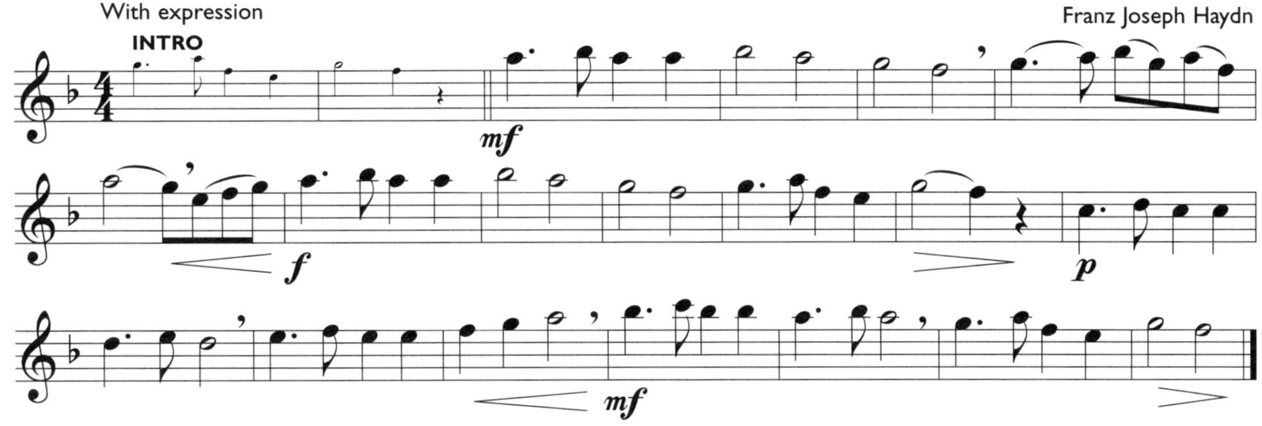



**2 Saint Anthony Chorale** (HARMONY PART 1 – FOR DUET, TRIO, OR ENSEMBLE PERFORMANCE)

**3 Saint Anthony Chorale** (HARMONY PART 2 – FOR DUET, TRIO, OR ENSEMBLE PERFORMANCE)

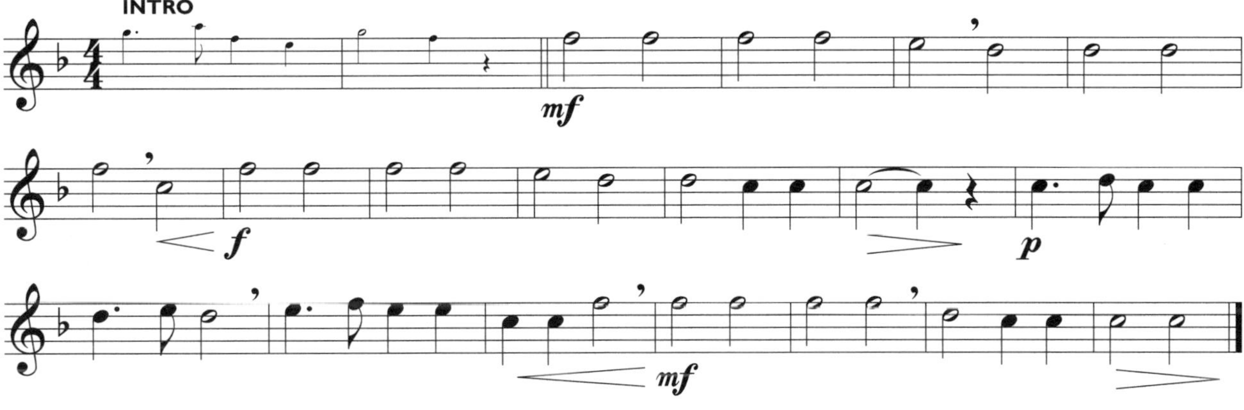



**4 Saint Anthony Chorale** (BASS PART – TACET)

Play Along
Tr. 98
Choucoune (THE MOCKING BIRD) Duet
Lightly
INTRO
Haiti
1a
2a
Have you heard the song of the mock - ing
1b
2b
bird? Have you heard the song of the mock - ing bird?
1c
2c
When you sad and blue, Then he mock at you, He sing high a - bove, And he laugh at love,
1d
2d
Oh I heard his tune by the Hai - tian moon, When I lost my Chou - coune.
NEW TONE:
B
Accom. Tr. 99
Can Can
Lively
INTRO
Jacques Offenbach
1.
2.
1.
2.

# AURAL TRANSPOSITION
## A Musical Assessment of "By Ear" Playing Technique[1]

### AMERICA

Samuel Francis Smith
Henry Carey

**Assignment #1:** Learn to play this fragment of *America* starting on **C, F, B♭, E♭, and A.**

**Assignment #2:** Learn to play the entire song starting on **C, F, B♭, E♭, and A.**

### THOU, POOR BIRD

Round

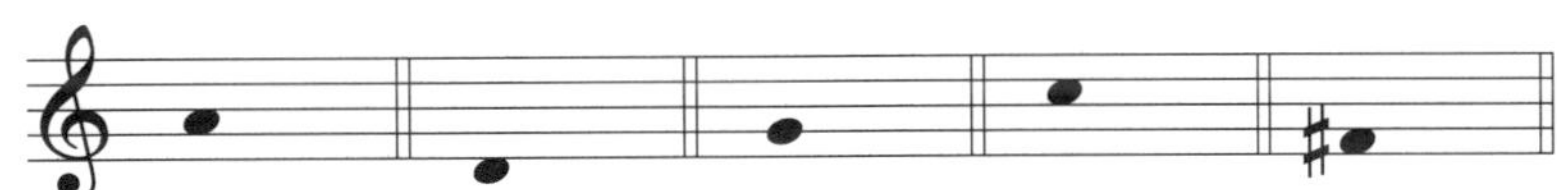

**Assignment:** Learn to play *Thou, Poor Bird* starting on **A, D, G, C, and F♯.**

### MARY ANN

Calypso Song

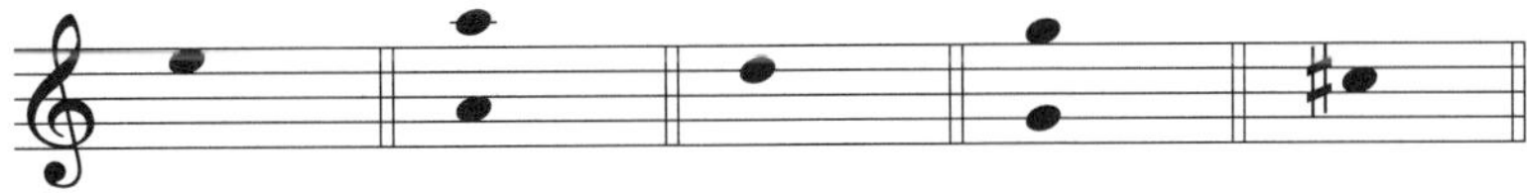

**Assignment:** Learn to play this fragment of *Mary Ann* starting on **E, A, D, G, and C♯.**

---

[1]Excerpts taken from *Studies in Aural Transposition* (Froseth, M442). www.giamusic.com

# SCALE ROUNDS IN MAJOR
## A Musical Assessment of Technical Skill

### #1 - 4-Part Round in A (C Concert) Major

# SCALE ROUNDS IN MINOR
## A Musical Assessment of Technical Skill

# RESOURCES FOR SELF-DIRECTED PROFESSIONAL DEVELOPMENT

## Movement to Music Skills

- A prerequisite to the development of music listening, reading, writing, performance, and conducting skills

- A form of aesthetic experience

Resource: Froseth, James O., Albert Blaser, and Phyllis Weikart. *Music for Movement*. Book and compact disc. Chicago: G.I.A., 1993. M-189BKCD

Resource: Froseth, James O. *Move to the Sound of World Music*. Compact disc. Chicago: G.I.A., 2006. CD-668

## Rhythmic Verbal Association Skills (Phonetic Rhythmic Syllables – Froseth/Blaser)

- A vocal language that codifies rhythm

- A way to think intelligently about rhythmic patterns that you hear

- A means to musically dictate rhythm

Resource: Froseth, James O., and Albert Blaser. *MLR Verbal Association Skills Program Part One: Rhythm*. Compact disc. Chicago: G.I.A., 1999. MLR-378CD

Resource: Froseth, James O. *Rhythmic Flashcards Set One*. Includes compact disc. Chicago: G.I.A., 1998. MLR-421

## Melodic Verbal Association Skills (Solfége - Kodaly Movable Do)

- A vocal language that codifies melody and harmony

- A way to think intelligently about melodic patterns and harmonic progressions that you hear

- A means to musically dictate melody and harmony

Resource: Froseth, James O., and Albert Blaser. *MLR Verbal Association Skills Program Part Two: Melody (Solfége)*. Compact disc. Chicago: G.I.A., 1999. MLR-379CD

Resource: Froseth, James O. *Melodic Flashcards for Recorder*. Includes compact disc. Chicago: G.I.A., 1998. MLR-489

## Melodic and Harmonic Ear-to-Hand Coordination Skills ("By Ear")

- The means to transfer what is heard, recalled, or imagined to instrumental performance "by ear" without the aid of music notation

- A foundation skill for music memorization

- A foundation skill for music modeling

- A foundation skill for music improvisation

- A means to musically dictate rhythm, melody, and harmony

Resource: Froseth, James O. *Performance-Based Ear Training: Studies in Aural Transposition*. Book. Chicago: G.I.A., 1996. MLR-442

Resource: Froseth, James O. *Performance-Based Ear Training: Performing Patterns and Scales 'Round the Circle'*. Book and compact disc. Chicago: G.I.A., 1994. M-424/425/426/427/428/429/431/432/433/434 (books) AND M-451 (compact disc)

Resource: Froseth, James O. *MLR Melodic Ear-to-Hand Skills Program*. Audio cassettes. Chicago: G.I.A., 1985. MLR-408

Resource: Froseth, James O. *MLR Harmonic Ear-to-Hand Skills Program*. Audio cassettes. Chicago: G.I.A., 1985. MLR-400

Resource: Froseth, James O. *MLR Harmonizing Melodies Ear-to-Hand Skills Program*. Audio cassettes. Chicago: G.I.A., 1985. MLR-399

Resource: Froseth, James O., and Albert Blaser. *Do It! Improvise!* Compact disc and booklet. Chicago: G.I.A., 1994. MLR-422

Resource: Froseth, James O., and David Froseth. *Do It! Improvise II! In All the Modes*. Compact disc and booklet. Chicago: G.I.A., 1995. MLR-424CD

## Aural and Visual Diagnostic Skills

- The essential prerequisite to remediating individual instrumental performance problems

- A means for diagnosing and correcting ensemble performance problems

Resource: Froseth, James O., and Michael T. Hopkins. *Visual Diagnostic Skills Program*. CD-ROM. Chicago: G.I.A., 2004. M536 (brass) and M537 (woodwinds)

Resource: Grunow, Richard F., and James O. Froseth. *MLR Instrumental Score Reading Program*. Workbook and compact discs. Chicago: G.I.A., 1982. G-2313 (workbook) and G-2313CD (compact discs)

## Teacher Self-Assessment Skills

- The essential means to become "aware of what you are unaware of" in the classroom, studio, and rehearsal hall

- The means to take control of your professional development in the classroom, studio, and rehearsal hall

Resource: Froseth, James O., and Molly A. Weaver. *Music Teacher Self-Assessment: A Diagnostic Tool for Professional Development*. Videocassette and manual. Chicago: G.I.A., 1996. MLR-444

# ALTO SAXOPHONE FINGERING CHART

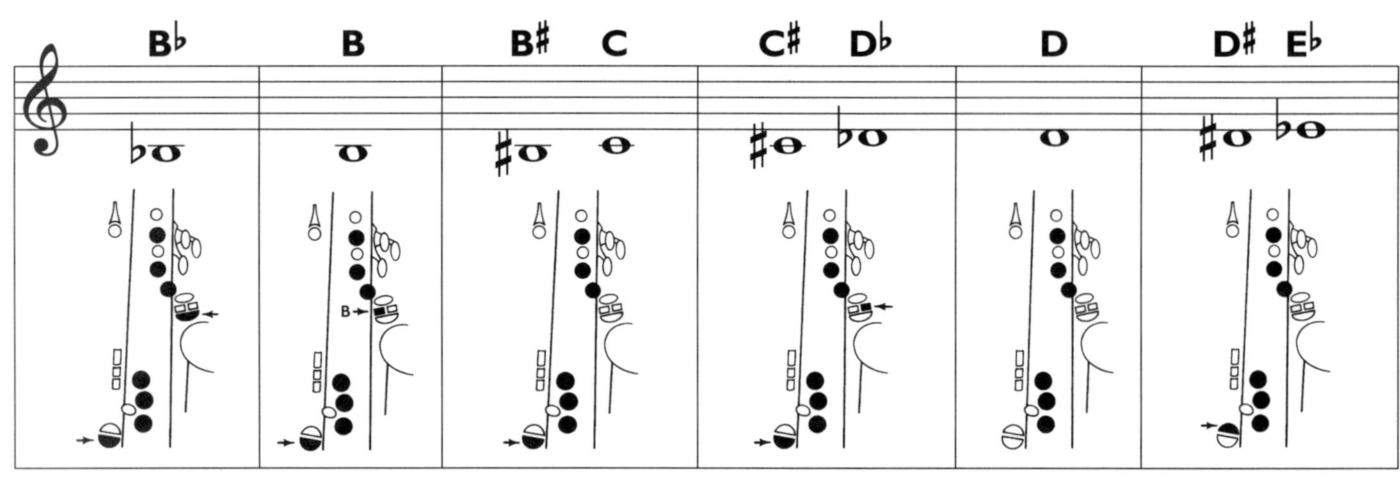


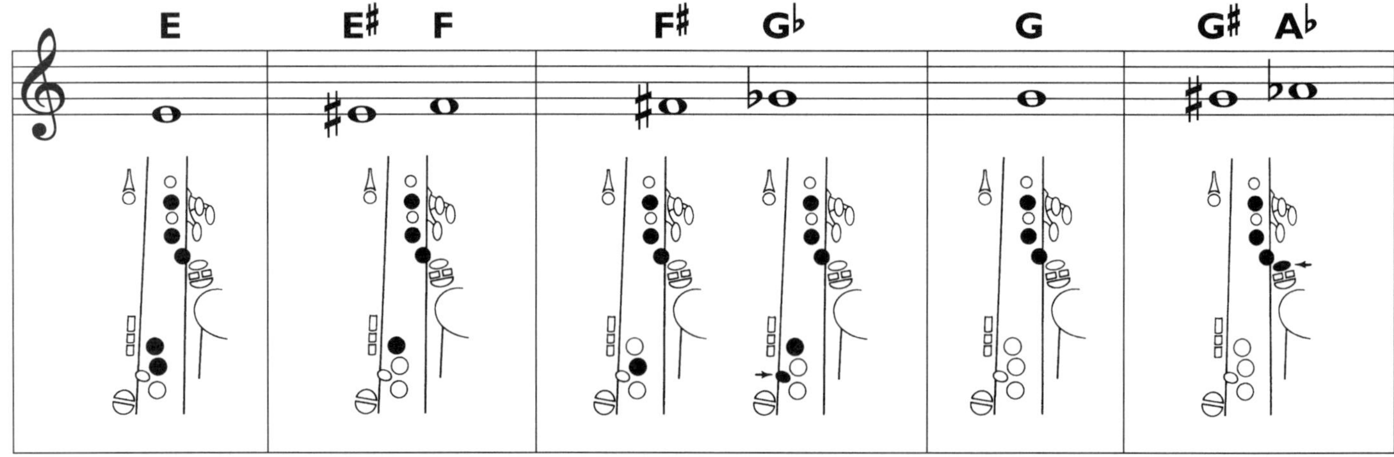


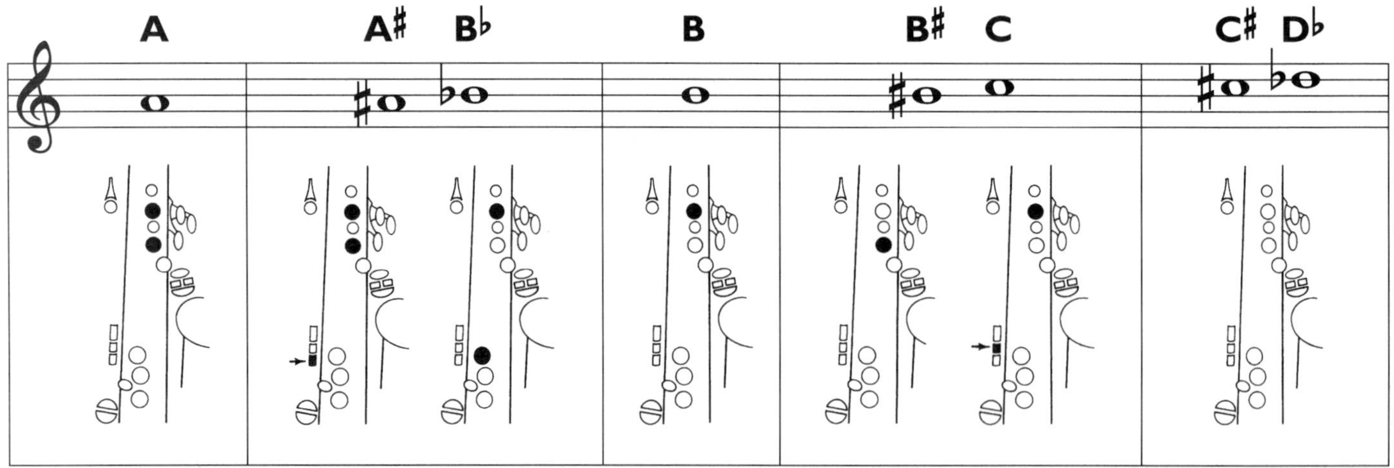


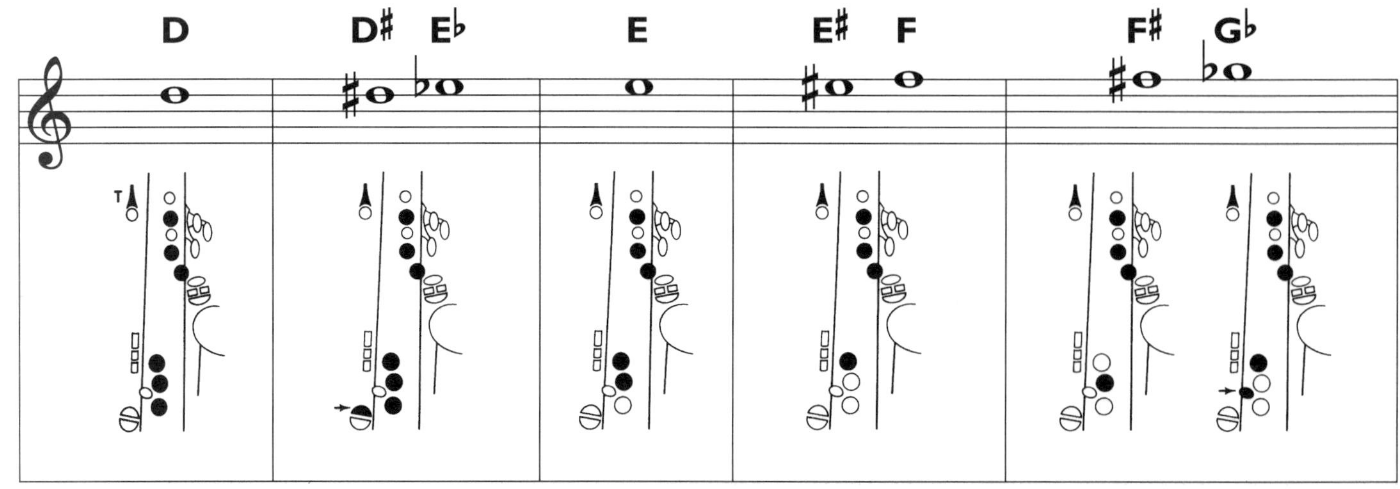

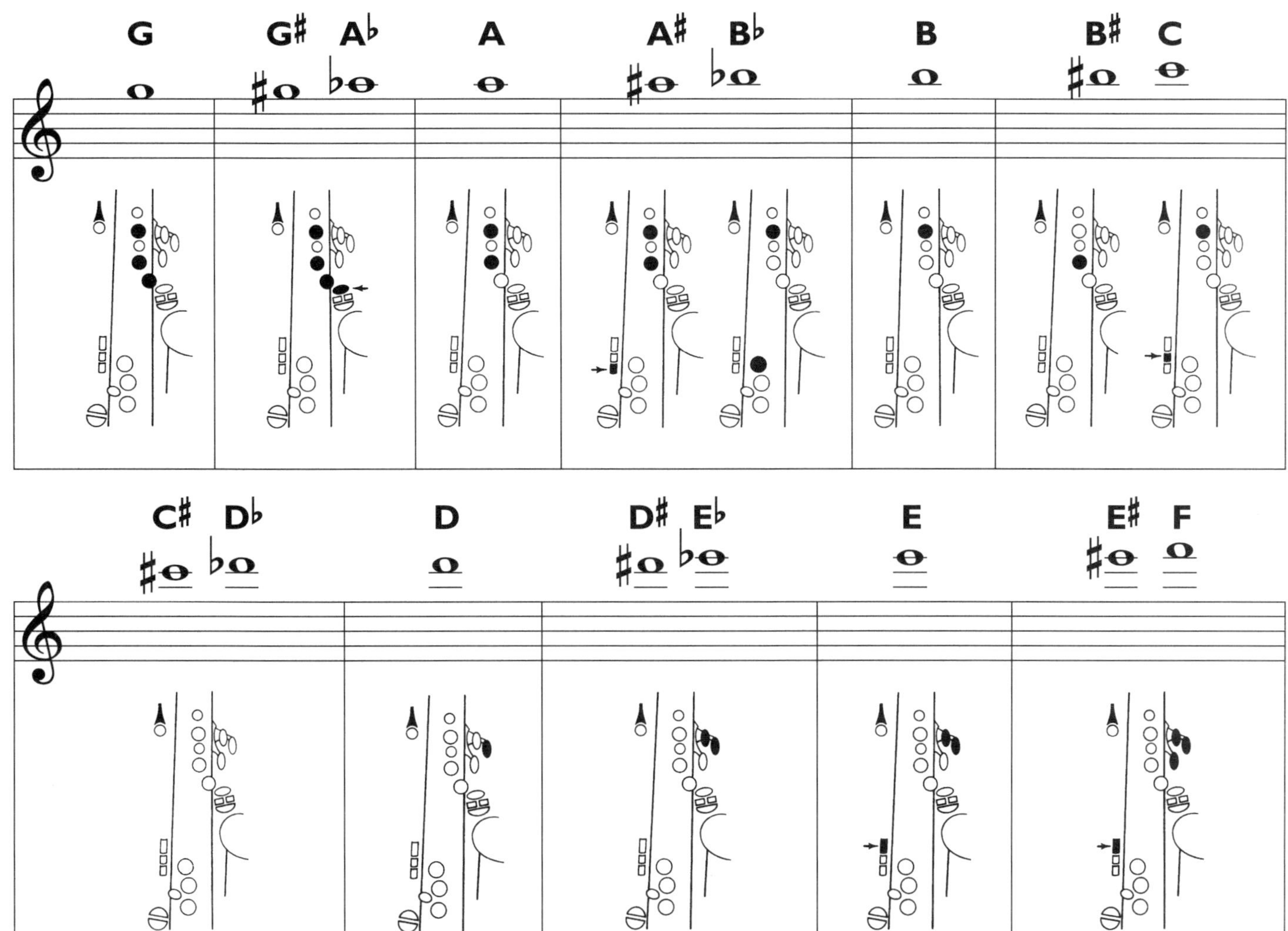

G
G# Ab
A
A# Bb
B
B# C
C# Db
D
D# Eb
E
E# F